TAROT
LIFE
LESSONS

"Julia Gordon-Bramer is my go-to tarot reader (affectionately, 'my oracle') and lifelong friend. Her insight, both profound and precise, has been a guiding light for me and many of my friends. I am excited for anyone to experience her artful wisdom, whether through this book, a reading, or her next magical offering."

NICHOLAS PETRICCA, LEAD SINGER AND FOUNDER OF THE BAND WALK THE MOON

"*Tarot Life Lessons* is as entertaining as it is educational. If you know nothing or very little about tarot, by the time you finish the book, you'll know a great deal. If you're a seasoned reader, you'll find fresh insights to expand your 'tarot brain.' Julia Gordon-Bramer's book is a gem among tarot books."

TERO GOLDENHILL, AUTHOR AND JUNGIAN TAROT GUIDE

"As you enter the private journals of Julia Gordon-Bramer, a seasoned tarot card reader, prepare for a transformative journey. This captivating book might challenge your perceptions but will leave a lasting impact on your life. Open yourself and allow these intimate narratives and experiences to reflect the profound guidance of tarot on your personal path!"

DR. HARMONY, AUTHOR OF *TWIN FLAME CODE BREAKER*

"*Tarot Life Lessons* weaves together Julia Gordon-Bramer's extensive experience as a tarot reader and her personal Fool's Journey. This combination provides a unique learning tool unlike any other tarot book I have read. Although I have been using tarot cards for many years, I found myself diving deeper into the meaning of the

Major Arcana cards and expanding my knowledge with each story she shares."

NADINE GORDON-TAYLOR,
CREATOR OF *CRYSTAL CLEAR ORACLE*

"Julia Gordon-Bramer highlights the major cards of the tarot deck and explains them in a most entertaining way via stories about clients. It's part memoir with a lot of spilled tea about people and their dreams, disasters, and enlightening tidbits about tarot, where it came from, and how it uses religious references. A fun, fast read!"

SUSAN MCBRIDE, USA TODAY BESTSELLING
AUTHOR OF *BLUE BLOOD*

"This isn't just a well-crafted prose journey but also a discerning deconstruction of prevalent misconceptions like the tarot being solely about predicting the future. It unveils the tarot's true capacity to facilitate a profound journey into the subconscious, thereby equipping readers to better navigate the ebb and flow of life's challenges."

SHAI TUBALI, AUTHOR OF
UNLOCKING THE 7 SECRET POWERS OF THE HEART

"Gordon-Bramer connects the multifaceted meaning of the Major Arcana to engaging examples that embody each card's unique energies. Each timeless archetype comes to life in stories gleaned from her many readings with clients over decades as a professional reader."

WENDY VAN ALLEN, AUTHOR OF *RELIGHTING THE CAULDRON*

"Julia Gordon-Bramer has been an exciting guest, talking tarot and reading her tarot cards live on various radio shows I've hosted for many years. I have been continually surprised by her accuracy and wisdom!"

TONY COLOMBO, PROGRAM DIRECTOR
AT NEWSTALKSTL 101.9 FM

TAROT LIFE LESSONS

LIVING WISDOM
FROM THE
MAJOR ARCANA

JULIA GORDON-BRAMER

Destiny Books
Rochester, Vermont

Destiny Books
One Park Street
Rochester, Vermont 05767
www.DestinyBooks.com

Text stock is SFI certified

Destiny Books is a division of Inner Traditions International

Cataloging-in-Publication Data for this title is available from the Library of Congress

ISBN 978-1-64411-817-7 (print)
ISBN 978-1-64411-818-4 (ebook)

Printed and bound in the United States by Lake Book Manufacturing, LLC
The text stock is SFI certified. The Sustainable Forestry Initiative® program promotes sustainable forest management.

10   9   8   7   6   5   4   3   2   1

Text design by Debbie Glogover and layout by Virginia Scott Bowman
This book was typeset in Garamond Premier Pro and Gill Sans with Carilliantine and Nexa used as display typefaces

To send correspondence to the author of this book, mail a first-class letter to the author c/o Inner Traditions • Bear & Company, One Park Street, Rochester, VT 05767, and we will forward the communication, or contact the author directly at **JuliaGordonBramer.com.**

For Tom
and with gratitude to all of
my tarot clients

CONTENTS

*

AN INTRODUCTION

To open this book is to enter my private journals as a professional tarot card reader. Are you ready? Warning: *it might get personal.* Personal to me. Personal to you. Another warning: *it might affect how you live from this day on.* Tarot is like that. Some of these are real-life stories that I recorded on a tired, bleary-eyed night at the end of a long amalgamation of readings given to party guests. Other chapters are the struggles of regular clients that have troubled me awake in the smallest hours of the night or lessons I have learned with strangers as we laughed over coffee and cards one afternoon. Sometimes the card I am writing about was part of a client's reading, and sometimes the stories reflect the themes represented in the card. Because the tarot has built-in symbolism, I have matched each of my stories here to a card, starting with card number zero, the Fool, the place where we begin. I am not a guru, and I am not a counselor, but after forty years of reading the cards, I have learned a thing or two about people, where they come from, what and why they do what they do, and where their energy is headed. I have learned that no story is unique. These are human stories. My story is your story, just with some different details.

Perhaps you do not yet even know what the tarot *is.* Maybe you presume I'm a conjurer of spirits or channeling something supernatural. Maybe you think I'm a mentalist with a talent for observation and guessing correctly. You might have seen a deck of tarot cards in movies and books, often in the hands of a traveling fortune teller or mystical old woman. I hopefully don't fit those depictions of a decrepit crone quite yet, nor do I want to come across as the trickster. Let me first say that it would be hard to conjure spirits doing a session at a noisy party, a crowded Starbucks, or over the phone, which are my main venues. I don't use ghost hunting equipment as we see on too many television shows. It is not uncommon for people to meet me for the first time and exclaim, "Oh! You look like a normal person!" I *am* a normal person, just more sensitive to others' energies than most, and with an unusual occupation.

Here's a quick history lesson. Tarot was first conceived in fourteenth-century Italy as a game for royalty and the wealthy with loads of leisure time, probably a minute percentage of the population. This was during the Crusades; lore tells that, under the guise of play, the cards' symbols, pictures, and numbers worked as a code to keep secrets related to magic, astrology, alchemy, numerology, and even dangerous political ideas off the radar of the repressive church government of the time. In the following stories, you will see how these cards remain timelessly valid for people today. Whether or not the romantic legend of vagabond travelers smuggling mysticism underground throughout Europe by tarot is true, the cards today are used chiefly for divination, the practice of seeking knowledge of the future, and especially for personal growth.

I love my work, even if others dismiss me as a joke and corporate friends think I can't sustain a "real" job. Oh, I've had more than a few of those jobs, and I spent many hours of my younger years chasing down the dollars in an office cube. I can do that work, but it is not the truth of me and not the best use of my talents. Being a tarot card reader is less about being clairvoyant or a fortune teller and more about understanding the abundant symbolism and spiritual exposition revolving around and within the cards, and how one might take the cards' advice to better one's life. When my younger son still lived at home, he would occasionally eavesdrop on bits of my sessions over speakerphone. One day he proclaimed, "You are kind of a counselor, Mom." That is true. Others might call me a life coach. Call me a spiritual GPS, or even mom, if you want. Call me whatever you like.

Let's begin with the ordering of the tarot. The first twenty-two cards, called the Major Arcana, represent the key players and milestones in life, the sacred adventure from birth to death. Those are my primary focus in this book. The remaining fifty-six Minor Arcana cards explain the mundane, day-to-day stuff, and you will see how these contribute to the bigger picture. Altogether, these seventy-eight cards tell the human story. Much of the tarot is logical and psychological. I often compare it to dream analysis, revealing subconscious beliefs and motivations in many colors, numbers, symbols, and pictures. If you've ever read anything about archetypes or the initiate's journey by mythologist Joseph Campbell or psychologist Carl Jung, you'll recognize some of those themes in the tarot.

You have probably seen some of the more famous Major Arcana cards in popular culture: the wise old Hermit, who graces the inside cover of Led Zeppelin's fourth album, the Fool, with his standard playing card equivalent of the Joker, as well as the Lovers, the Wheel of Fortune, and the Death card, which are just some of the Major Arcana images to appear in James Bond movies, video games, pop songs, novels, television, and more. The remaining fifty-six cards, the Minor Arcana, are in suits, like modern playing cards. Instead of Hearts, Clubs, Diamonds, and Spades, however, the tarot has Cups (for matters of love and emotion), Wands (for energy and creativity), Pentacles (for money and career), and Swords (for ideas and action).

So how does tarot work? The combination of pictures, numbers, symbols, and signs on tarot cards, interpreted by the tarot card reader, reflect the subconscious and explain our experiences, in the same way dreams express what's going on inside and outside of us. You trust that the right cards will come up for you—or you don't, and you learn that they will come up anyway. That's the beauty of it: you don't have to believe, and it will still work for you. You don't have to be all that knowledgeable or wise to experience transformation with tarot.

It only takes a certain amount of familiarity to decipher a world full of meaning in the cards. I maintain that anyone can read tarot cards with time, a little bit of guidance, and the drive to evolve and live more deeply. As you read on, you will see in this book that I am not the only one reading the cards; my clients often help me by applying what I glean from these symbols and pictures to their situations. You will also notice that I, too, learn and grow with each client's experience. I trust that the right clients come to me, without exception, that they are there both to receive help and, sometimes, to help me as well.

I've been a writer and a reader for a lifetime, so it makes sense that I would love the tarot. Within each card is a little story. You will soon see how the cards are imbued with mythology, Biblical parables, archetypes, and spiritual advice. These cards work together to illustrate the human experience. Some people use the tarot only for fortune telling, only asking what will happen, and I think that's a waste of its power. The tarot is a tool to awaken and tame the subconscious, to help us grow our strengths and make changes when we identify our weaknesses. It's a way to conquer problems and move on from painful situations and the baggage we carry through life. Each tarot card has different meanings, whether they fall right side up or upside down. Upside down is called a *reversed* position. The person's question and the layout, or *spread,* I use also help determine the card's meaning. There are no duplicate cards. The miracle of tarot is how the right cards show up, time and time again, to provide guidance or to illustrate someone's story. People marvel all the time, telling me that I explained something "*exactly* as it occurred," or that "He would have said those very same words," or ask, "How could you have known *that?*" Let it be known that I don't research my clients. I don't ask for pictures, birthdates, or even last names. I don't fish for information, and when I'm doing phone readings or email, I cannot be tipped off by hints from facial expression. The truth is that I don't know anything about what I see. I'm just the messenger, reporting back from Elsewhere.

The sessions you're about to read about may be sad, or joyful, or shocking . . . and everything in between. I write from my perspective, but I do not judge. We are all human and capable of so much, good and evil. I strive to pull away the dark curtain and expose the Great and Powerful Oz of the supernatural not as a giant godhead to be feared but rather as the Source, of which we are all equally a part. My own stories are interwoven with those of my clients, as our experiences together have often been powerful and even life-changing. Being a professional tarot card reader has been an adventure, to be sure, and the first story we begin with is my own. I like to think that as a tarot card reader I play a very small part in working to heal the world. With any luck, maybe one or some of these stories will contribute to that work within your life. Or maybe you'll just have a good time reading them.

***

Names and identifying facts have been
changed to protect client privacy.

0
THE FOOL

I grew up with the Bohemian surname of *Svolba*. However my childhood did not resemble the itinerant traveler pictured on the Fool tarot card, with his traveler's satchel and a little white dog at his heels. No, even with my central European roots reaching back to those mystic drifters, tinkers, and tramps, becoming a professional tarot card reader had never been a part of my life plan. Maybe Fate decides these things for us. Whatever the reason, somehow, this oddball career of mine evolved, possibly due to spiritual energy, God, or karmic debt.

The Fool card begins with the number zero, representing nothingness and an absolute beginning. The Fool has no value and represents both the outsider and the Everyman (or woman or person). He is at a starting point. I started when I picked up my first tarot deck at age sixteen. I was a hippie kid in the 1970s, not a true hippie of the '60s, but a copycat, preferring Jimi Hendrix and Led Zeppelin when disco was the rage. A *ragamuffin,* as my British Nana referred to me, my looks being part of my adolescent rebellion. So there I was, a long-haired stoner who had blindly wandered into a magic shop, looking for nothing in particular, wasting time one hot Maryland summer afternoon in an air-conditioned mall. This was not a New Age shop—those places weren't around in the 1970s. No, this store was a Houdini-type place with tables full of gags and tricks and novelty items. And there, in the glass case beside all of the fake wands, sponge balls, and flies in plastic ice cubes, was the first tarot deck I would ever see.

As the Fool makes his route west through the snow-covered Alps, his head, like mine was then, is happily in the clouds. His card embodies air, that number zero, and also the Cosmic Egg, which birthed what scientists today call the Big Bang. He is the first breath of life and the last dying breath. In some illustrations, the Fool follows a butterfly, another creature of air and wind. Like the teenage me, the Fool has no plan or destination as he steps forward. His feet are on the ground for now. He does not see that he is about to step off a cliff. No one knows if this is just a small step or a drop that will swallow him up forever . . . the way that tarot swallowed me.

"Do you want to take a closer look?" the saleswoman asked me. I say "woman" here, but she was maybe twenty years old, tops. Still a girl, but grown-up to me back then. Until that time, my concept of a fortune teller was strictly from the movies: the haggard old sorceress in a caravan casting a long, bony finger over her oracular crystal ball. Yet here was a lovely, hip mentor, with her shoulder-length golden hair, her bangs in a trendy feathered cut, brushed away from almond-shaped eyes, and a gauzy Indian blouse as loose and flowery as the Fool's garb. The young woman seemed to be serene, or whatever I might have conceived serenity to be at that age, and she appeared to have all the knowledge of the universe within that finger-smudged plexiglass counter.

I suddenly became aware of my drab, straight hair, parted in the middle and brown as dirt. Anyone could see that I clearly lacked mysticism, wearing an orange t-shirt with a Paul McCartney and Wings decal, an iron-on from a family trip to the Ocean City boardwalk. I wondered if I was fit to own tarot cards. What does someone who buys tarot cards *look* like? Do they carry a magic wand? Wear a flowing gown? A crown of stars? Did other tarot card owners look as average as me?

She *had* asked if I wanted to hold them. Had I heard her correctly? After a long pause, I said, "Sure." I hardly believed that I would be allowed to touch something so fantastic.

My shopgirl mentor slid the cards out of the box and thumbed through them, and she told me that the tarot is used not only to read people's fortunes but also as a way to understand ourselves. She said that, unlike all the rest of the merchandise in the store, tarot is not a trick. Tarot is a kind of magic that is real.

Real magic? Sign me up! I bought them on the spot, maxing out my paltry babysitter's budget. Following the young woman's directions, I wrapped my deck in a silk cloth, which the store also conveniently happened to sell, as magicians go through loads of scarves. She recommended that I store them in a wooden box, and I knew just the one—an old container my mother once used for flour in our kitchen. I had swiped it years earlier as a coffer for things precious to me: newspaper clippings soaked in tears over the Beatles breaking up, hard candies, favorite jewelry, and a postcard of Big Ben from Nana in Great Britain. I knew on a deep level that this particular box was infused with my personality, although I would never have used such words back then. Operating from sheer instinct and practically no history of my own yet, I knew that this box fit the precise requirements of Real Magic.

The Fool has no knowledge or experience. Everything is play. That's where I was when I had to figure out *how* I was supposed to use these things. The lexicon of tarot readers made it all the more confusing. What was *divination?* How did one get direction and insight? I started with the little white paper instruction booklet that came in the package. We call these LWBs in tarot circles, and there is respect for them as each deck has its own. Looking back, I think that learning by the LWB was a great way to start. It was not laden with description or intimidating to read, and it gave my intuition space to grow.

"You're very good at this," my friends told me. I soon became everyone's favorite party guest.

The Fool embodies the child within us all and symbolizes that we are all born pure as we begin our journey in life. The tarot was structured on something called Qabalah's Tree of Life. On that tree, the Fool connects the point of Wisdom to God. But Wisdom on the

Tree of Life refers to the wisdom of the world, which God considers "foolishness."*

Even my mother will tell you that I was a pretty mystical kid. At around eight years old, I hummed self-composed magic songs and created secret rituals where I threw chestnuts wrapped in my handwritten stories and poems into our family's burning fireplace in winter. I'd wrap them all in my father's carbon paper sheets from his 1970s-era office supply cupboard for extra power. I had a passion for carbon paper as it doubled and tripled my words. I knew that the smoke would lift and carry my words off somewhere else, somewhere greater. Maybe the smoke and flames from the crackling wood would deliver them to my dead grandfather, whom we called Pampa. A black-and-white photograph with Pampa sat on our mantel above the fireplace, him holding me as a baby on his lap in the center, the two of us flanked by my mother and Nana. He had gone on to become an angel, I decided. Or maybe my words would travel on the air across neighborhoods to a boy I loved but dared not speak to. I regularly pocketed what I deemed magical stones and herbs, creating my own spells. I made everything mean something—how could it not?

Or maybe my mysticism began when I was twelve, lying on my back in the summer grass, instinctively learning to meditate alone in the dark, to find that halfway place between awake and asleep. There, it was only me and a canopy of stars. Sometimes, just like in the picture of the Fool, I had the company of a little white dog, Muffin, who watched me curiously.

I would say: "Look, Muffin, there is Mars, rising near the moon . . ." or "That bright star is Jupiter, my November planet. . . ." Muffin would lift a white floppy ear and cock her terrier-mongrel head, confused. The white dog on the Fool card represents our innocent, animal nature before we left the primeval Garden of Eden.

In my teens I read books on astrology. The sky spelled alphabets, revealed pictures in constellations and meteor showers, and

---

*I Corinthians 3:19 in the New Testament of the Bible.

diagrammed the way things would be and the reasons. It was like learning to read. I got the gist and major points by immersion into a new language in which I was not yet fluent.

I wasn't entirely pagan, though; I was active in our Episcopal church, which had its share of charismatic Christians, including those who spoke in tongues. They had me spellbound, and a couple of words even came to me, although I never felt consumed and taken over by the Holy Spirit in the manner that those people did. Our church group elders were in their thirties, played guitar, and knew how to speak to the teenagers on the fringe like me. Under their tutelage, I read and studied the entire Bible, and it was on a church retreat where I learned automatic writing, going off alone to allow God to speak through the pen. Of course! The *pen* would be my way into the spirit! After all, "In the beginning was The Word, and the Word was with God, and the Word was God," says the Book of Genesis. God was *words!* Of course, of course. Here was a God that made sense.

I read books on dreams, graphology, mythology, numerology, and Jungian psychology throughout those teen years. I learned about different religions and how alike they all are at the core, rivalrous siblings descended from the same lineage but with differing dogmas. It fed my spirituality as I came to see the interconnectedness of everything.

Looking for signs and symbols in my suburban 1970s world became an everyday, natural experience. My tarot cards became a life decoder and a compass to navigate and reduce the chance of bad luck. Ideas and actions became airy Swords. The world was made of earthly Pentacles, of which I never had enough. My wet, watery, adolescent emotions were Cups, and my wild and enthusiastic Sagittarian energy could only be expressed through the suit of Wands. My ideas and action were Swords. Everything in life was contained within those pictures, and although the card characters' fashion was medieval, the people, faces, and expressions are eternal and universal. There are always youths and wise old men. There will always be mothers, fathers, lovers, and warriors. Animals. Work. Sickness and death, parties and birth. The Wheel of Life turns for us all. I saw parents and teachers I knew in the faces and characteristics of the Kings, Queens, and Emperors of my deck. My friends and I were all mere Pages, just children, with dreams of becoming Knights, finding our fortunes, and riding out victoriously on horses or in chariots, preferably with radial tires, good gas mileage, air conditioning, and a stereo, into lives of our own.

I mastered the meaning of numbers: the solitary rank of the ones, the partnership of twos, the creativity of threes, and so on. I began to understand that everything was charged with sacred meaning if I wanted to believe it, and this meaning, for me, was lifesaving as my personal world often seemed too terrible. Back then, I used the same coping mechanisms as many teenagers who are highly sensitive and don't have the emotional tools to manage: drugs, alcohol, sex, and other methods of self-destruction. Or maybe I just did the seventies. Later, when I was in my twenties, my now-ex-husband joked, "You have personally experienced every topic on the talk shows, except not knowing your sexual orientation." He was right. And I had friends who went through that one, so close enough. The Fool tries everything and commits to nothing. The Fool hangs out on the cusp of living and dying. In time, I learned that all of my vices and personal problems had been gifts, and they helped me connect to, understand, and sometimes help others in similar places without judgment, condemnation, or pity. All of my struggles made me stronger, but I would not realize this until later in life as a professional tarot card reader.

Around the age of sixteen, I began to have premonitions. They were mostly very random and seemed to have no real importance. I had just acquired my driver's license and drove my little sister to the mall in my rust-covered 1974 Mercury Comet, a death-trap I purchased for $300, my life savings, from a boy at school. As I sat there in the driver's seat behind a peeling blue vinyl steering wheel, I had a vision of a big black crow on the side of the road with a broken wing. It was a waking dream. I thought to myself, "Why did I think of that?" And then, a few minutes down the road, I saw that crow in real life, exactly as I'd thought it. The light glossed its dragging wing in tints of blue, its battered mast. While I grieved that this dark bird was injured, that helping it was hopeless, my foresight strangely thrilled me. I learned much later that to us mystics, the crow indicates magic, prophecy, transformation, and the onset of creation. He was a perfect totem for a Fool like me, a first sign coming from the still undeveloped blackness of the void. Symbolically, the crow flies between the worlds of the living and dead, in the same way the Fool joins the beginning and end of life in the tarot. Other visions came and went over the years that are now forgotten, but that crow stayed with me forever. I can't be sure which came first, the tarot deck or the premonitions, but I perceive them as connected in my memory as if they happened on the same day. I doubt that they did, but I am sure that this was the age when I stepped through a portal and became someone else.

I drifted away from any open spiritualism for a few years but studied meditation and metaphysical thought quietly on my own. Then, after a ten-year marriage and two kids, I divorced and turned back to the trusty cards for direction once again. It was the worst time of my life, and so I risked financial security and my professional reputation for some fun, as any Fool would. I started an alternative music magazine in the 1990s. I led my team and myself through business and personal decisions using the tarot. Tarot readings were how we usually closed our staff meetings and opened our parties. I sought out more and more books on the subject. The tarot cards were continually there as life went on but always on the sidelines. I did what most intuitives do: put my psychic energies on the back burner, raised my children, earned some money, and returned to school. Reasonable stuff, the things required for living in the world. But whenever I was stuck or confused, I'd pull some cards in an attempt to understand the history of, say, the stray cats I rescued or for advice as to if we should trek to Chicago to attend Lollapalooza and who should come along. I dated and eventually married again. I got a bachelor's degree, went corporate for a while, and then earned a master of fine arts degree in creative writing in 2010. At school, I used the cards as icebreakers, as

I was a significantly older student in a class of twenty-somethings and didn't at first feel like a part of the gang. I read for my fellow students and professors around class periods and at semester-end parties. One professor even brought me in as a guest to read cards for some of his other classes.

"You should do this for a living," he said.

"Will you do this at my party?" more and more of my friends asked.

I shrugged. It had always been a hobby. Nothing to take all that seriously, but then what does the Fool take seriously? I was self-taught, never credentialed by any esoteric school or academy. But I had become wiser through reading and experience. My card reading became more and more well known, and people wanted me at their events. After a few long and exhausting nights of working for free, I decided that yes, I would charge for it. It was only fair. Besides, I think it was all divinely orchestrated so that I would be available for other efforts: the work of my life.

The Fool of the tarot is often linked to the troubadours, or wandering minstrels, who traveled around Europe knowing the power of words and who kept the pagan goddesses alive through poetry and song. While in my own poetic schooling, I discovered that the world-famous poet and writer Sylvia Plath, who called herself a pagan, had a tarot deck of her own, and—surprise!—she had constructed her poetry collection *Ariel* in perfect alignment with the tarot. Tarot was the cipher to unlock meanings within her poems in a system never before grasped. You may laugh, but I believe that Plath wanted me to uncover this treasure. She, someone, or something redesigned my life and guided me to become a professional tarot reader, which allowed me the money and freedom for this writing and research. Why me? I have no idea, but there had been hints and mystical correspondences scattered across my life: I was born nine months after Plath's death. We shared the same German-Polish paternal background. My grandmother's name was Sylvia. My maternal grandfather and her father both lost their left legs. I lost my grandfather when I was eight, the age at which Sylvia Plath lost her father. My mother was British, married an American, and stayed here. Plath was American, married a Brit, and stayed there. It goes on and on. I call it my very own "Lincoln-Kennedy Coincidence," if you've ever marveled over that historical weirdness.

But this book is not about Sylvia Plath, even if she steered me here. This book is about my mysticism and the tarot. Yet I can't help mention her because it was through Plath that I cut my teeth studying Qabalah, alchemy, mythology, astrology, history, and the various religions that interested her across her lifetime. As the Fool blindly steps into the abyss, I often puzzled over what I had fallen into. Just as the established church government mistrusted the wandering minstrels and poetic troubadours, I am viewed today as an equally seditious figure in academia. Could I handle the terrible criticism and resistance that the old guard held against me, a tarot card reader who dared to publish scholarship? During the Crusades, the troubadours/Fools were cast out by the established church because their poems and songs gave women power; the church's goal was to eradicate thousands of years of goddess worship and make women subservient. And I am an outcast because I present a woman's brilliance with her layers of mysticism, while the white men in tweed jackets and bluestocking women insist upon reading Plath literally, and merely as a suicidal hysteric.

I relate to the Fool, who is also correlative with a royal court jester who gets away with saying and doing irreverent things. The Fool challenges the untried and the untested in life, breaks the rules, operates unconventionally, and eventually acquires the wisdom needed to accomplish goals by experiencing every stage from zero to twenty-two, the World, the final card of the journey of the Major Arcana.

These days my free time and money are spent on books, conferences, lectures, and hanging out in library archives hunched over journals, letters, scrapbooks, school papers, and book annotations for hour upon hour to seek enlightenment and prove my theories. I remind myself that it doesn't matter if most of the world does not get it. Like the Fool, I do my work for sheer joy. I do it because, like in

Plato's "Allegory of the Cave," I have seen the light, and I can't shut up about it.

Over the past decade, I began to study Buddhism and the Tao and to read and practice *A Course in Miracles*. I embraced the work of Neville Goddard, who reinterprets the Bible not as historical fact but to be used as a manual for creative visualization. Some of my more fundamentally religious friends dropped me, believing I'd gone too far into the dark side. Some of my atheist friends thought I went bonkers, taking Plath's dual position of both shunning organized religion and yet being highly spiritual. All of the teachings I devoured seeped into my tarot readings, and they inculcated me further into mystic initiation. For instance, the Hanged Man card became a contemplative Buddha, and the Nine of Swords holds the subconscious truths we don't want to face. As the Hermit is forever on a solitary, introspective quest that leads others with his lantern, I learned that each card not only embodies the fundamental meanings I studied long ago in the LWB, but that the cards are tools and present opportunities for practical spiritual guidance. Each card is transformative, and every one of them can change your life.

Academia, for me, has been a hell of egos and horrors, some as subtle as quiet unfriending on social networks and others as bold as sabotaging my projects and opportunities. The traditional grown-up world has not been much better, with judgmental looks and barbed opinions over my unorthodox alternative rock lifestyle, my abandonment of the corporate world, and, of course, my unconventional spiritual practices. Am I Satan's plaything for a laugh or the Chosen One, I sometimes wonder. I know I have also been chosen for tarot, however, because that business grew without trying.

After a few years of reading tarot professionally, local television and radio invited me on, and soon I was doing spots on Nickelodeon and MTV. But reality TV taught me that I'm not skilled at faking emotion in retakes. I can still hear the twenty-something MTV producer:

"Can you do it again, but with more, you know . . . mystery? Can you say it, like, you know, like you're casting a spell?"

"Er . . . I'm sorry. I'm *not* casting a spell, you know. That feels kind of . . . stupid. I have to say it how I mean it because I'm actually doing this for real."

I thought that was the end of my short but glorious television career, but opportunities have kept arising. I'm willing so long as I don't have to conform to a false script and can do this legitimately.

The truth is that I tend to speak my mind, even when it pisses people off. I take my work seriously, maybe too much so. And while yes, I am both a spiritual and a practical person, with one foot in the mystical water and the other on the dry land of paying bills and making a living, I can't and won't put on a fake show for the camera. You see, tarot often has still moments, which can be dull to viewers at home. There are times when I don't do much more than stare and ponder its susurrus of messages and endless watery depths.

I'm not entirely boring, though. The Fool is spontaneous and in constant movement and change. So am I. Catch me in the middle of a tarot reading, and it's also not unusual to see my eyes well up with tears, hear me shriek with laughter, or toss out a few cuss words. I don't hold anything back. It depends on who I'm reading for and what their energy is. I'm a mirror. I reflect their thoughts and feelings back to them. And somehow I have gotten rather famous locally. I joined the ranks as one of St. Louis's Top Ten Psychics and CBS Radio rated me St. Louis's Number One Fortune Teller. I'm a regular during afternoon drive time on St. Louis's most popular talk radio show. I've had features on Show Me St. Louis and Great Day St. Louis, TV news profiles, guest spots on all the radio stations, and coverage in *St. Louis Magazine,* the *Riverfront Times,* and even the *St. Louis Business Journal.*

Spiritual work can get rather exhausting. I'm co-opted, yes, but I'm not possessed. I didn't always know how to leave my readings for others behind and just live my own life. For many years, undergoing the emotions of others could be too much. When I was about eighteen, I flew from D.C. to Chicago to visit relatives who were at the height of alcoholic and codependent dysfunction. My friends told me that I "wasn't right" for weeks when I returned. I learned much later on about how to protect myself. Obsession, martyrdom, and sacrifice aren't my thing. I have tried that too many times.

There are some professional tarot associations out there, but no "ivory tower" credentials bestow a Ph.D., or even a bachelor of arts, in tarot. I am an expert from life, from more than forty incredible years with the cards now, and I am successful because I tell the truth and give direction, rather than just predict the future. I will shock and shake people awake if I have to. I've lived a lot of lives along with my own. I know that sometimes a tarot reading can be restorative all by itself, to be seen and heard, and to share the hard stuff. Sometimes, when others experience healing, it also heals a part of me.

It wasn't until the 1990s that we began to hear the term *empath* to describe over-feeling people like me. Before then, I just thought I was weird. The Fool gets called that, of course. He is portrayed as a jester, joker, or juggler in some tarot decks. Like me, he is the party entertainer but rarely an invited guest. In some decks, the Fool is a madman. He is forever a peripatetic vagabond and outsider. As number zero, he does not really belong anywhere, not in the Major or Minor Arcanas. This seems a little bit sad and entirely accurate. Like me, he's not categorically in entertainment or academia, and it's awkward.

I'm hanging out on the edge of the road with the trickster crow. The Fool is about to fall, to step off a ledge, and that's appropriate too because to take on another's feelings is the sensation of sinking into oceanic fathoms. To read someone's tarot cards is like tumbling helplessly in love with someone for a few minutes or even drifting off to sleep—before you slam your hands on the mattress to break the fall you were taking in your dream. Except that, unlike when I am in a dream, I am aware enough to know that I am not actually living, or re-living, my clients' situations. And they, meanwhile, learn that they are not alone in their brokenness—we are all broken in places. Sharing these wounds begins recovery and makes us stronger. There is something about their stories that is also mine. The details may be different, but we share the same emotions. Tarot shows us all a path to make things right, giving us hope.

People have labeled me "psychic" and I'm a little uneasy with that title. I'm intuitive, and like the Fool, I know that all things are possible. I don't want to be fettered by labels with built-in baggage and assumptions. If I am psychic, I'm not the kind of psychic who walks into a room and knows a person's name, history, or birthday. I've met some of those types, and it's an impressive gift. Nor do "I see dead people," to use a phrase from a movie, although I do occasionally catch a few interesting images in the corner of my eye or see fleeting reflections in a mirror. Despite my adolescence, I'm not super New Age and smiley all the time, all "Blessings upon you" and "Namaste." Nor am I the next Tony Robbins with a silver tongue of motivating platitudes. Plenty of my friends probably think I'm a bit too dark, in fact. I do it differently. Like the Fool, I'm not fixed in any specific direction or belief. I'm open. I'm just me, with my tarot cards, which are my key to understanding you because you and I are one.

At the time of this writing, the Earth has traveled around the sun fifty-five times for me. I'm at the halfway point. I know this because I had a vision: I saw myself old, frail, and in a wheelchair. My sons stood beside me, and they were old men in their eighties, at least. Because of this vision, I am sure I will live to see 100 years, and I'm guessing it'll be closer to 110. Let this mark my words.

Who am I when I am not connecting with my clients? When I am not the positive and negative titles of everything I am or have been: wife, mother, scholar, rock and roll journalist, ex-wife, stoner, or alcoholic? Who was that magical kid? Who's that reader on radio and TV? One tarot card opens the door to the next, taking us through the phases of life. I'm going to luxuriate here in the Fool's neutral world a bit longer. The Fool sees every moment as a new beginning. He has no past and infinite potential; he enjoys the journey of life and does not know his destination until he arrives.

The majority of my clients become regulars, at least for a while, and therefore they feel like friends. My highest purpose, the reason I am on this planet, is to help others attain their best selves as I continue to find my own way. We will discover our directions and grow together. Some days I comfort with love; on others, I will call you out on your shit. I know that I will relate with everyone who chances upon me on some level. We are all working out this crazy life business together. I am everyone. We are all one, and we span generations, countries, and families.

My father used to say our family name was Bohemian, with its colorful caravan of sociopolitical baggage as wanderers, thieves, entertainers, and mystics. His people originated from a central European country later called Czechoslovakia, once partially annexed by Nazi Germany and now peacefully broken into two republics. Our ancestors, who came to America in the early 1900s, were immigrants from land with ever-changing boundaries. My DNA kit labels me as being of Polish and German descent on my father's side, English and Welsh on my mother's. The Travelers were everywhere in Europe and all through Wales, where my mom was born. I am a spiritual wayfarer, by blood and by belief. Our family never identified as Romani or used the word *Gypsy* to describe our heritage, even before that word was considered a racial slur. Yet I can't help but hear the words of Sylvia Plath's poem "Daddy" in my head as she speaks of our shared roots of mysticism, history, and love of the cards:

> *With my gypsy ancestress and my weird luck*
> *And my Taroc pack, and my Taroc pack.* *

I was born to read tarot cards; they are a part of me. Sylvia Plath showed me that much. When we are ready to go in any direction, like the Fool, we drop our limits and rules. Do any of us really know who we are and where we are going? Let me show you now where I have been.

---

*Taroc is another name for tarot cards.

Buying Your First Tarot Cards

Someone once told me that tarot cards are more powerful when given as a gift.

Ridiculous. Don't fall for superstition like this. You're a child of God, remember? The cards are whatever you want to believe they are. Choose a deck with designs that speak to you on an artistic and emotional level. It is bound to be more powerful.

Experiment with several different decks, but in the beginning, please understand that LeNormand and oracle decks are different systems. Learn one method at a time. Also, watch out for those tarot decks with gorgeous Major Arcana designs (these have historically been called the *trump* cards, but Donald Trump seems to have changed the vibe of that word) but very plain Minor Arcana cards. Plain Minor Arcana cards, also called *pips*, are considerably harder to read until you're an expert. In my opinion, a Rider-Waite tarot, or a design based on the Rider-Waite such as the Universal Waite, is the best deck with which to begin learning.

THE MAGICIAN.

1
THE MAGICIAN

Reading tarot cards is a headlong plunge into another person's life, an instant kind of intimacy. Maybe this is the experience a musician has when they move another person's body with music, or that of an artist, emotionally stirring someone through the creation of images, or a what a psychologist feels upon coaxing a patient into a breakthrough.

I get to do all of that. I love people, and I become a part of them for a short time, and they know they are understood. I adore connection and finding that common place with people. Loving people like this is different from infatuation, which, as we all know, can get obsessive and unhealthy. We've all been to the place where our hearts are stupid and powerful enough to override common sense, and all we want is to feed that obsession. It doesn't matter what age we are or how much life experience we've got. Our hearts can trick our heads into believing that we have found love, and we want so badly to believe that it's real.

My client Veronica got tricked. She was an attractive and polished senior citizen with hair in a sensible short bob, dyed chestnut brown. She wore the kind of jeweled and appliqued designer running suit no actual runner would ever sweat in. She met me for a reading in my neighborhood Starbucks, where the baristas all know me (I tip them well and give them free readings so that I may claim this place as my office away from home).

The Magician invariably presents well and endeavors to entertain, enlighten, and assist, and to call the power of the Heavens down to the Earth. At their best, Magicians have talents that not everyone else has. People declare the Magician to be "amazing!" As a tarot card reader, I embrace being a Magician in the most positive sense of interpretation. How do the right cards appear, without duplicates and in the correct position, time and time again? That's the mystery of tarot. I do not claim this magic as mine. That is a God thing, and I am just the channel.

At the coffee shop, Veronica found me first, identifying me by the small wooden treasure chest I held, which contains my tarot cards. We claimed a two-person table against the wall. I give my clients a choice of several different styles of tarot decks, so I asked her to choose one. Veronica's thin, freckled hands grabbed the *Joie de Vivre Tarot,* shuffled the cards, and handed them back to me. I laid the cards out on the table.

"Your King of Cups is in reverse, crossed by the Lovers card. The love life feels like a problem," I said. The air in the Starbucks was full of that enticing coffee aroma calling to her: *Wake up!*

"Yes," she admitted. "My husband, Michael. . . . " She trailed off, taking a sip of her grande decaf before telling me that he had passed a year earlier. The Hermit in reverse shadowed over her life: she was afraid of being alone. In her present, however, was the Magician in reverse. Uh-oh.

I have known some Magicians in reverse. We all have. The Magician, in reverse, is the sweet-talking, handsome man who promises to call after a one-night stand. The Magician, right side up or upside down, is a conjurer, practicing evocation, the summoning of spirit. He's clever and he captivates. Some Magicians are in the light and some are not, depending on how the card falls. Some magical grimoires offer that the Magician has made a deal with the Devil for his talents and abilities. (For myself, I like to think that I have surrendered to God for my gifts, and the more of my ego I drop, the stronger my talents become.) In the present day, we see the Magician in reverse all the time as the begging addict with a dramatic story about why he needs "bus money." The Magician in reverse is the liar you need to trust because if you're right, you're helping him, *and* you're a kind person. And if you're wrong, he's evil, and you're a sucker. Who wants to go *there?*

"Veronica, do you know who this character is?" I asked. "Because he is trouble."

"It's probably a man named Chris," Veronica said with a sudden laugh.

I've never studied body language or how to tell if someone is lying, but when people laugh like that, I know things are not as casual and easygoing as they make them out to be. Veronica knew already that she was headed for trouble.

She continued, "I met him online. Can you tell me some more about him? He is *very* good looking, and he has been texting and messaging me." She widened her eyes and gave a wide smile. When one asks about a relationship, I have learned there is usually doubt beneath the question; when you're secure and safe, you don't think to ask.

It caught me off guard that a woman from her generation would jump into the digital world on her quest for a new mate. But why not? She was a youthful seventy-seven, and she told me she wanted a younger man. She said that men her age could not keep up with her, which made me chuckle inside—I envisioned her lounging seductively in a negligee, calling the shots to some young hunk. "Plus," she said, "I do not want to be a widow a second time around. No, sirree."

We all love the Magician when his card falls upright. He is the life of the party and charming, and he keeps everyone spellbound. In reverse, his skilled sleight-of-hand illusions make it so easy to have faith that he can do anything. I added some cards to Veronica's already busy spread to elaborate on this Magician in her life. I saw that "Chris" was a man with no conscience: pure selfishness represented as the Devil card reversed, and the Seven of Swords reversed said that he was looking to take advantage of her.

The famous psychoanalyst Carl G. Jung wrote that tarot archetypes have been with humanity since the beginning of time and they tell all of our stories, consciously and unconsciously. That's what makes the tarot so powerful. Every society's got liars and thieves among them, and the Magician in reverse is their calling card.

"Chris and I met on Facebook," Veronica volunteered with a blush.

"Things have gotten pretty intense, and we have fallen in love." This vulnerable expression made her look even prettier, and it made me hurt for her all the more.

There were no cards of love showing anywhere. Not even earnest friendship was on the table. The Magician puts on *such* a marvelous show, but it's smoke and mirrors. I took a sip of my latte, and diplomatically, I began to suggest that perhaps she was the target of a scam artist.

"Veronica, do you think that maybe you're just looking to find someone for companionship because you're still missing your husband? You're lonely, and I'm worried you're not selective enough. I'm worried that . . ."

She bristled. One is never comfortable being told they might be wrong and, worse, that the person she loves is not a decent guy. The pretty, vulnerable look disappeared and her jaw stiffened. I stopped my words and took a different tack:

"Veronica, no one person is entirely innocent or corrupt, and I am not saying that Chris is pure evil. I just want you to be careful because this kind of Magician doesn't believe in himself enough to dare to make things happen honestly. Remember how the superheroes in cartoons and comics say, 'Crime doesn't pay'? It doesn't. That's because crime comes from faulty energy. See, at their core, the crooks have no confidence in their ability to succeed forthrightly. *You* are looking for love from a place of loneliness . . . well, that's faulty energy. It's like you're calling problems toward you. Bad energy begets bad energy."

Veronica looked at me with amusement. "Are you comparing Chris to a supervillain?"

She totally missed the point.

"Um, not exactly. What I mean is that nothing good can grow from a no-good seed, and as you sow, so you shall reap, as they say. That's karma. Since you're looking for love out of loneliness and not joy, your energy is also not going to pan out. Follow me?"

She looked a little perplexed.

"Think of it like this," I continued. "Mother Teresa said, and I'm paraphrasing, 'If you invite me to an anti-war rally, I'm not interested. If you invite me to a peace rally, I'm first in line.' You want to make your decisions based on what you want, not what you don't want. I'm concerned that you're approaching this relationship from loneliness and therefore attracting trouble. Regarding Chris's energy, I'm convinced he is not honest with you. Please be careful."

"There *are* some things about Chris I wonder about," Veronica said. "We only talk in email and instant messages. He won't Skype or Facetime or even talk to me on the phone. Do you think that's weird? But oh, Julia! He is so handsome! You should see his pictures. Sometimes he *sexts* me! That is something I would never have done in my single days before Michael. Chris is younger than me too, and he says that I am the most beautiful woman he's ever seen. . . ."

Her eyes gleamed at the flattery as she told me. Chris, or rather the idea of this lover, gave her ego a much-needed boost. Veronica refused to let common sense cloud her judgment of Chris. I wondered how many other lonely widows this Chris was talking to. The Magician, right side up or upside down, does his best work in front of an audience. He was born to put on a show. Straight up, he is plainspoken and articulate, often a gifted communicator. In reverse, he is a master at telling others what they want to hear.

"Chris is an admiral in the navy," Veronica continued. "On his Facebook page, when he sent me the friend request, I saw his ship, which reminded me so much of my Michael, who, you know, was also in the navy . . . but not an *admiral!*"

Oh, God. A busy admiral had fallen in love with a woman he doesn't know on Facebook? I didn't think so.

"Yes, Veronica. I *do* think that it is weird that this powerful, successful grown-up man won't Skype or talk to you on the phone to have a true relationship. Veronica, please believe me. I have nothing vested in this either way. You know that. With all of my being, I am positive that Chris is hiding a great deal from you."

"He says he will do a phone call or video with me eventually, Julia. The problem is that it's never a convenient time. He's busy, you know. He's a very important man."

"Does he live here in St. Louis?"

She shook her head. "Chris is in Texas when he's not on the ship. He's planning a trip to St. Louis, but he's unsure when. He has promised that he will meet me in person soon, and we'll take vacations together wherever I want to go and stay at all the best hotels."

By now, I had set the cards aside and recapped to her what I had just heard:

"So Veronica, this admiral in the navy has said he loves you, but he has never met you in person and has never even talked on the phone, Skyped, or FaceTimed with you. . . ."

"Yes, but we text all the time!"

I softened my voice. "Veronica, I'm eternally talking to my younger clients about text relationships. Texting isn't true communication. It's playing at communication; a person cannot be known outside of bona fide, in-person experiences. Not even with the help of tarot cards. I know it looks convincing when you see photos and a digital profile, but that's just the side he wants to show you. It's not all of him, if there is any veritable *him* at all. Veronica, if he genuinely loved you, he would want to see you, every chance and every way that he could. So this, to me, is suspicious. And I have to say that his cards make him look like an out-and-out liar and thief. I am afraid that you're going to get hurt. See the Magician on this card? He shows up well. He presents himself as a magic man. But it's not magic. It's a trick."

She looked away.

I thought about how the stage magicians say *Abracadabra!* This incantation, which comes from ancient Hebrew, means *I will create as I speak.* Chris was all words, no creation, as far as I could tell.

I continued. "Veronica, I know that I am supposed to answer the questions, not ask them. I don't want you to think I'm fishing for information. But I need to ask you something serious. Has he ever asked you for money? For any reason? Even just a little bit?"

"Well," Veronica began with a smile, proud of what she was about to tell me, "he was overseas in Afghanistan and did not have access to his funds. A Shah friend was getting him a gorgeous handmade wedding dress covered in jewels for *me* to wear! He asked me if I could wire him $11,000 and said he will pay me back when he is stateside."

"Oh, no. You didn't give it to him, did you?"

"Of course not. I don't have that kind of money lying around. I told him I'd have to pawn my wedding ring and some other jewelry to get that much together quickly."

"And you *won't* do that, right?" I asked, gritting my teeth and praying.

"I haven't decided," she said. "Chris promised that he'll get the ring back out of hock later."

That was such a Magician-in-reverse thing to say. Damn that Chris. I also felt sad and angry at Veronica for being so gullible. How many others are preyed upon like this every day? How many senior citizens lose what little fixed incomes they have because they only want to be loved? I thought about how, almost daily, I get Facebook friend requests from these fake military guys with handsome photos and statuses of "widowed" and "single."

Right side up, the dashing young Magician has all the tools on his table to make magic, and he does it successfully and with confidence. But in reverse, it's all a sham. The altar we think we see is actually a swindler's table, the cards are marked, and the dice are loaded.

"Veronica, look at these cards, OK?" I put some down, knowing that any cards that showed up would do. This tarot spread was going to agree with me. The Universe would not let me down for her sake.

"There's the Five of Pentacles. See those poor beggars on it? Veronica, he wants to take all your money. You'll never meet him. You'll never see him in person. This is probably some guy in an African phone bank working several other lonely widows. He knows how to flatter you. He knows the right things to say. The Magician has all the tools on his table to create the illusion he wishes. See this Seven of Swords, with the picture of that guy sneaking off with all the stuff? He is going to rob you blind. And look at you, in this Nine of Swords! You will end up crying alone in the dark."

That was maybe a bit of an overdramatization for that last card, but I had to get through to her.

I looked at Veronica's face and saw that she was upset, hearing this news she did not want to hear. But she was a grown-up, and she had to listen. Damnit, I was going to *make* her understand how harmful it was. I wanted to reveal what an egotist the Magician in reverse is and how little he cares about what happens to her, so long as he gets what he is after. This was the Light Magician against the Dark. However, I had to do more than pull away a curtain and say *Presto!* This was not coins and scarves and a rabbit in a hat that we were messing with; this was her heart.

"Look here, Veronica, there is a Queen of Wands reversed with whom he's in cahoots. He's probably living with a woman and running this operation to rip off American widows looking for love. Don't give him one red cent, Veronica. Please, I beg you."

Our hour was up. I could have gone on forever. I'm sure that Veronica felt that I had.

A lemniscate, the infinity symbol, is drawn over the Magician's head in the tarot. This symbol is a Mobius strip considered to have only one side, which has the mathematical property of being unorientable. Stage magicians use Mobius strips to create the illusion of magic. Chris was one-sided and all illusion.

That night, I went to bed troubled. This sometimes happens when a client is on my mind. Sometimes I get enmeshed and have difficulty letting go. Lying in bed in a half sleep, the place between dreams where all the spectral messages enter, I saw golden orbs whirl around me. They were wheels of light, wheels inside wheels, with insect legs and wings and many little eyes, and faces, each different: distorted faces of lions, humans, birds, and chimera. The sound of their wings was like the rush of water. They frightened me a little. I could compare them only to aliens I had seen in a 1980s Hollywood movie called *Batteries Not Included.* But these were smaller and more insect-like, although they were decidedly mechanical. They were metallic and glowing in golden illumination, a tiny flame inside each one. Or maybe they had huge flames inside them, and I had lost all perspective on their distance. They were too radiant to look at directly for very long, and my eyes began to tear up. They lowered their wings and became still.

"Why are you here?" I asked.

"We are praying for you," the beings told me; I understood them through an inner means, not hearing voices but just knowing.

"Why me? There are far worse cases. Tonight I am praying for Veronica. Pray for her."

"We are all Veronica," they said.

Of course. It's so easy to forget that we are all one, and everyone just wants to be loved. I forget all the time. I had slipped into the Magician card, straight-up, with his cocky overconfidence. I had taken on the job of trying to fix everything, but that wasn't what was asked of me. A tarot reading was all she wanted. We sympathize with others. We feel smarter, which is a false superiority. We think we know better and that it is our job to fix someone else. I had to look at where I still hurt from the times I had been in love, how I was triggered to care for her more than I probably should have.

Veronica phoned me the next week and ended up becoming a regular client. Much to my delight and approval, she gave up on Chris, realizing that something was too fishy. Yet for the next several months after our first meeting, she called me every week or so for phone readings to check out the next man and the next. These relationships were almost all fake social network schemes, and all began on Facebook. Every gorgeous gentleman, usually in the military, needed money for various urgent reasons with promises to pay her back. I made Veronica promise me that she would never give any money for any reason to anyone she did not know *in person* for at least a year or more.

Veronica became more and more exasperated with me. "You sound like my *daughter*," she said in protest. It wasn't a compliment. "You girls don't understand, Julia. I'm not out and about the way young people are. I don't work a job and meet people. Online is the only way I can meet anyone these days. And it's safe."

Was it? I could not and would not attempt to fix Veronica. I had to mind my own business. It took great restraint to hold back. I would be there if she needed me, and I would offer advice if she asked. I sent Veronica a text message the next day, checking in.

"Everything's fine," she said, in a tone that shut me out. After all the spiritual work I had done over her, that hurt a little. I laughed a little then, knowing that I had done this work also for myself, and my feeling of hurt was just ego stuff. Veronica was a grown woman who would do what she wanted. I was her tarot card reader, not her daughter or even her friend, although I perhaps mistakenly thought I could be the latter. I could not protect her from herself, and she would learn her lessons as she needed to.

The next night, in the darkness of my bedroom and in deep meditation, I asked the spirit beings to return to me. The lucid dream began.

"Can you talk to me again? Maybe leave me with some wisdom?" I asked.

They gathered around me and took me to the edge of an abyss. This void of darkness was blacker than anything I had ever seen. It was outer space with no planets, no stars. Pure nothing.

"Watch," one of the creatures directed me. It positioned itself upon the edge and then let its wings drop. Then, it fell in. Soon it was gone from sight.

I waited there with the remaining creatures. It seemed like a long wait, although who knows how dream-time is measured. "And . . . ?" I asked. "When does it return? It's coming back, right?" I had grown fond of the little guys.

"No, it's gone," they told me in unison without a hint of emotion.

"Forever?"

"Yes."

"What does this mean?" I could not accept it. This so saddened me . . . I felt nearly in a panic.

"It means that nothing matters."

This, of course, is Buddhism 101. The world is only an illusion, the Magician's domain. It is an outward reflection of what is in our minds, and so nothing in the world is real. Nothing is real but Love. Still, I had grown from being afraid of the strangeness of these little beings to loving them. And we are all One, and so it was also a part of me that fell into the abyss. Even if only in a dream. Was this a dream? Something else?

It was something else. It could not have been a dream because this became one of my greatest lessons about consciousness.

The next day, while reading some news on the Internet, I happened upon a work of art from the 1800s: Ezekiel's Wheel, a portion of the *Thrones: Christ in Majesty* fresco found in the St. John the Baptist Church in Kratovo, Macedonia. I sat stunned, looking at that part of the painting for ages, with its intertwining golden wheels studded with many eyes and wings. I made it my wallpaper background on my computer, where it remains today. I searched for other artistic renderings of this Bible story. Of course, I went right to the Book of Ezekiel and read the details of this vision that the prophet recorded, which was so near to my experience, except that I saw only the wheels and not the Lord God behind them. Maybe next time. Or maybe I will see it all when I am worthy. Perhaps every artist who has painted Ezekiel's wheels has seen them too.* I am blessed to be among such company.

The Magician stares straight ahead on his tarot card, lifting his wand high with his right hand while his left arm stretches out from his body, index finger pointing to the ground as if to distract the audience to look elsewhere. Where do we hold our gaze? In his eyes? At his wand? To that unknown place on the ground where he points?

Veronica could not break from the Magician's spell. The mystics advise that everyone we call into our lives, good and bad, is here to steer us upon our path. When Gandhi said, "Be the change you wish to see in the world," he didn't mean to be a model citizen. He meant that what we see outside is going on within us, and the best solution to help others is to fix ourselves. The Magician's hands, one toward the sky and one down to the Earth, represent *As Above, So Below. As Within, So Without.* We've all been deceived, ripped off. Sometimes we've also been the cads and the criminals, and we want to make amends. Dishonesty of any kind always comes back to hurt us. The universe doesn't know the difference between stealing a nickel, swindling thousands from a widow, or embezzling millions from a corporation. Chris and his ilk

---

*I have since learned that these angelic beings are called Ophanim.

will get theirs because their energy is corrupt. Because Chris didn't trust that he was enough to earn it honestly. And Veronica gets hers because she doesn't comprehend she is enough without a man, and she creates a world to prove it. It all just goes around and around again. Karma is indifferent. It's action and reaction.

What was I able to see in myself, as reflected in Veronica? Veronica taught me that I must have trust issues around love despite my now successful second marriage. She showed me the dangerous difference between sweet optimism and gullibility, two traits I am not a stranger to. And she showed me that I had taken the superior position of trying to reroute her path when it was not for me to be her navigator. It would never have worked if I had tried, as acting from a place of upset would be negative energy. As distressing as it is to watch, a tarot card reader can only call out that there are icebergs or abysses ahead. The captain of the ship must steer it from there. It's a lesson we all have to learn: to drive our own lives and stay out of the business of trying to lead others'.

And like the little being that dropped into the void, Veronica chose her heart over her head and, I learned later, lost her life savings. Abracadabra. After that, I never heard from her or Ezekiel's golden chariot again.

How Do You Know If You Can Read Tarot?

- You must be the type of person who can meditate, be hypnotized, and/or slip into a dream state fairly easily. That said, you will NOT be in a trance while you're reading the cards (not usually, anyway).
- You must be able to trust your first impressions and gut perceptions. A surprising number of people cannot do this (and that's all intuition is, really).
- Tarot is very personal. Much of it is intuitive. There are no hard and fast rules. You will create what you need at that moment. What's right for you can't necessarily be taught or told to you— although some guidance helps at first.

THE HIGH PRIESTESS

2
THE HIGH PRIESTESS

In the way that our thoughts create reality, what began as a joke, or maybe someone's daydream voiced out loud, happened: MySpace parties popped up across the country. We all traveled and took over a city for a couple of days, haunting the restaurants, crowding hotels, and jamming up poetry slam nightclubs and writers' centers. I discovered this crowd online in the early 2000s, the Pre-Facebook naught-years when MySpace was the thing. We were poets who had banded together, posted, and wrote for each other. We were in each other's Top Eight profiles, and we were all in a dark place, some of us in darker locales than others. Like the High Priestess who sits between light and dark pillars, I was with them, but I wasn't truly one of them; they knew it, and I knew it. My decades of sobriety had made it impossible for me to enter their club fully. But I loved them all the same, and I loved their words, if not their worlds. Some of them liked my words, but they loved my tarot cards.

This time, we were in the Phoenix and Scottsdale area, a wealthy golfing oasis in the American Arizona desert. Rosy was a doctor among our online gang who had come to Phoenix for a medical conference. Like the High Priestess herself, single and successful, Rosy had her shit together, an anomaly in this bunch. Her evenings were her own at the palatial hotel resort, where her practice had paid for her stay. The hotel was a palace with its tall marble columns, and it had all the fixings to host the perfect summer party on the patio. As luck would have it, I happened to pass through town at the right time, piggybacking on my husband's business trip.

Our MySpace friend Clayton was also a sure thing to be attending. He lived there in Phoenix, for the moment, when he wasn't hanging out in L.A. or San Francisco. After I arrived, he turned up at the hotel with a couple of friends I had never met before and would never see again. Clayton perpetually needed drivers, as he had lost his license to drunk driving. But wherever he went, he promised to be enough fun that his friends obliged. Vera and Dan also came by, laughing and drunk before the party.

The High Priestess holds all of the secrets of the Torah on a scroll upon her lap, and she possesses the great mysteries of the occult. Unlike this bunch with their addictions and distractions, she is in total control. The High Priestess is also a woman of secrets, which fits, as most of us used aliases on MySpace. I was *either/or,* after my favorite Elliott Smith record that referenced Kierkegaard's treatise on hedonism versus the virtuous life. *Rosy* was a fake name; doctors don't want their legal names out there, especially online and associated with this crowd. Clayton went by *Love Destroys Love.* I can't remember what names Vera and Dan used, but I called them by their real names. Maybe they had always dared to be themselves.

Clayton was possibly the scariest person I had ever met. I called him "Love" to shorten Love Destroys Love and, really, for its strangeness. He was, of course, not anything like Love. On the previous Memorial Day weekend, Love and I first met at the Venice Beach get-together, an overload of (their) drinking, music, and debauchery with little to no food and even less sleep. That first gathering, we MySpacers had flown in from our various corners of the states. We met in the L.A. suburb of Silverlake to sign depressive poetic tags in Sharpie markers on what was known as the Elliott Smith Memorial Wall. The wall was part of a music store building, painted in colorful swirls, which the recently-departed rock star had been photographed in front of for his *Figure 8* album. We were all obsessed with Elliott Smith. Besides writing poetry, loving Elliott Smith may have been the prerequisite for admission to this club, and I did, and so I was in. But like I said, the tarot cards also helped.

The High Priestess is intuitive; she is the psychic of the deck. I have her image on the back of my business cards. I knew that I would recognize my friends, although no one had ever so much as shared a photograph. On MySpace, they used cartoons or avatars, never actually identifying themselves. But their words! Their words were so real. I would know.

On that initial introduction with the group months earlier in L.A., we made arrangements to meet at a Mexican restaurant in the late afternoon on an early summer day. When I arrived, there stood this guy, well over six feet, thirty-ish, skinny, chain-smoking cigarettes beneath aviator sunglasses and a mess of longish blond hair. Love. He was a drifter and an unlikely leader of this even less likely team. I knew that Love had a history of heroin addiction, but he'd kicked that. Now his demon was alcohol. Dan said he was worse with alcohol than he'd ever been shooting up. It was truly too bad because Love was a genius poet, an obsessive animal lover, and a vegetarian. Although one might not say he was classically handsome, he was so damned likable that he continually had a crowd of women around him. Were they girlfriends or fans? I'm not sure. I loved Love too, for reasons I can't quite explain.

"Love! You're here! It's me, Julia! Either/or! I knew I could rely on you to be here."

Love looked down at himself, feigning surprise that he was there at all.

"Yes. I'm here. I think. Although the only thing reliable about me is my lack of future."

He hugged me hello.

We slummed around in Venice Beach on that first lost weekend, talking, laughing, singing, and dancing as a roving, floating party. I watched them drink, and I read their tarot cards, a fast way to get to know people. I learned all their stories, the most interesting tales, of course, being about Love. There was the time he'd begged on the street for money to purchase a live goat and spare it from slaughter at a county fair. He held the animal in the back seat of a friend's sedan as it bleated, pissed, and shit its pellet-poop on him for the twenty miles they drove to take it to a farm animal sanctuary. This story countered the one about how he stole his mother's television to sell for junk when he was still using. Hopefully God would weigh it all out.

Now, we were together again, this time in Phoenix on a fancy hotel patio. As this was our second get-together, we recognized ourselves as friends in the corporeal world, not just the digital one.

The High Priestess on the tarot card wears a long flowing gown that dissolves into the water at her feet. She would have fit in well with the elegant couples in suits and long dresses who floated past. Fashionable lovers leaned over railings looking at fountains. The women were attractive, tanned, and jeweled. Almost all the men wore a jacket. And us? Well, I was presentable in a clean knit top and shorts. Love had traces of a black eye when he took off his sunglasses, and he wore a red t-shirt that read *Born-Again Heathen*.

"Why does he always end a pleasant evening in a fight?" Vera complained, looking over at Love with a kind of fond exasperation. Vera referenced some altercation that had happened the previous night; I only got a few details and decided it was best that I didn't know. Vera's boyfriend, Dan, was dressed solidly blue collar in jeans and a work shirt. Vera wore a gauzy sundress that appeared as if she had slept in it the night before. We grazed upon bountiful trays of complimentary appetizers that all the beautiful people dared not touch. Love had a mouthful of deviled eggs, washed down with vodka and cranberry juice. His only meal that day. Who let us in there?

"I have my tarot cards," I sang out, my hand holding the pack upward and teasing it out of my purse like a snake charmer coaxing a cobra. "Who wants a reading?" My collection of odd fellows circled the table.

Lovely Vera was first in her white nightgown dress. She'd taken the flowers out of the vase on the table and woven them into a crown for herself, and it looked quite pretty. The High Priestess wears a crown too; only her crown looks like great rabbitty ears with a full moon set at the center; both are symbols of the goddess Isis, the maiden, mother, and crone. Vera was still a maiden. In my mid-forties then, I teetered somewhere between the latter two.

The High Priestess's face is serene and without expression, and like her, the hotel staff did not seem bothered by our antics. Magically, we had become invisible. If we were creating a disturbance, they were giving us a wide berth and pretending we weren't there, like so many handle the homeless. Lacking jobs and fixed addresses, my friends weren't that far from being homeless, but I was determined to *see* them. I didn't want to tame or fix them. That was far beyond my power. I just wanted to know them, to give them the gift of saying that they mattered, to me at least. There was something about them that fascinated me. I wanted to find the truths that laid dormant inside their addictions because those things were inside me too, even if I did not act upon them. Because of their words, their poems, I had grown to love them fiercely. They had let me into their darkest places. I respected that.

At our reconvening at this gorgeous Phoenix hotel, the gang drank again. Heavily. It was amazing that some of them, like Love, hung around as long as he had for as hard as he lived. He had told us, through poetry, about his stepfather raping him and burning cigarettes into his flesh at five years old. About growing up on the streets. Me? At this time, I was more than twenty years sober and the mother of two young sons. To read his poetry was often almost more than I could bear. It was a miracle he had survived it at all and still had any kind of heart.

"There is a reason they call it *spirits,* Love. That shit can take you over."

"That's the point," he said. "I don't want to be me."

The High Priestess sits in front of a veil representing the hidden mysteries. Depicted on this veil are pomegranates, the mythological fruit that tempted Persephone to Hades. The same juicy crimson seeds decorated little tarts that our hotel food servers offered on silver trays. On the tarot card, these pomegranates are arranged in the Qabalah's Tree of Life design, which originates in Jewish mysticism. The Tree of Life is a blueprint for how the universe works, and the tarot is structured to reflect it. In the High Priestess's lap is a scroll with the letters TORA visible. The Jewish *Torah* means Law, and *Tarot* comes from this word and the Latin ROTA, for *wheel of life*. Qabalah sees life in cycles and circles. My friends in this circle had no blueprints, no general direction for their wheels, and they kept no laws.

One of my gifts is that I can see the best in nearly anyone. This, I think, is one of the secrets to my success because clients know there is no judgment, nor do I try to force change. It is my job simply to witness them. The High Priestess sees all, and the pillars on her card bear a J and a B, two of the three initials within my monogram. Seeing the best in everyone is also my greatest downfall, as I have been burned in my blind faith and trust. Even with Love, to whom, over the months he was imprisoned in Tent City, I dutifully wrote twice a week on prison-approved, print-stamped postcards (drugs can be hidden under regular peel-and-stick postage stamps). And for whom I later bought a winter coat when he was freezing in San Francisco—a coat he lost or destroyed in a fight almost immediately. Love Destroys Love.

Some psychic, right? Psychics are not known for reading for themselves too well. It takes great restraint to find the neutral, detached place between the outcome we want and the outcome we most fear. Most of us, myself included, at least dip a toe into the water of bias, so I generally do not read for myself or family members as I am too invested in the end result. That said, people do have the opportunity to change their outcomes with a heads up and so, in addition to making my clients feel validated, I can warn them if things look grisly ahead. It's transformative, sometimes. I held out hope that it would be transformative even for this gang. You never know if one of them might find something or someone worth living for. Corrections can come out of remorse. Depression and anxiety demand that changes are made.

Was I just sharing their emotions that night, was I channeling something, or was I possessed? I don't know. Like the High Priestess, I was an intercessor, a mediator between the human world and the divine. There are no manuals on being extrasensory, or at least there were none in my formative years. This night, I was all over the place, experiencing whatever came up within them, and we all spat it out in strange verse. Maybe hip-hop artists tap into the same thing.

For Vera, I first pulled the Temperance card reversed, then the Tower, and then the other cards tumbled out. I rambled my stream of consciousness verse in its almost-rhymes:

> *Invitations and exits convolute*
> *and your Chariot driver*
> *has a DUI.*
> *Girl, is your Seven of Swords a crime of the mind?*
> *Look, you've lost Temperance. You are*
> *your own Hanged Man: twisted, tied.*
> *Pondering that state of You*
> *as cruel, a thief, and a liar.*
> *Murderer* and *the victim.*
> *Martyr. A scapegoat with cutthroat.*
> *Your Death body is guilty of life,*
> *for all you've still got that is warm behind*
> *the Eight of Swords' bars of air-conditioned frost.*
> *The Eight of Cups says your red-winged angel will*
> *burn your bridge from now 'til then.*
> *You'll never learn*
> *that you've killed all your chances*
> *for* when.

I looked at Vera's face. She gasped, laughing and a little bit nervous, but there was also a tear in her eye. The cards had called her out on her self-destruction. I think that those were *her* words; I just happened to be the speaker. The poems and the tarot cards did not eradicate anyone's depression: they expanded, deepened, and lent it meaning. In the spirit of my reading, Love feigned a cockney accent and sang out a few bars from the chorus of the Sex Pistols' "God Save the Queen" under his breath: *Noooo future, no future, no future for you!*

Rosy, our host, was up next. She had that remarkable gift I never had of being able to tie one on regularly, still get up in the morning, and keep her life in order. Patients' lives depended on her every day. Her days could be sober, but her nights? Whatever. Rosy's cards showed her Devil of success, her efficient eights, her dreamy sevens.

"Give me a poem too," she requested.

Was that what they were calling my ramblings? I complied.

"All of these rings," I said of Rosy's success in the Six of Wands, which bore a laurel wreath, and then the Ace of Swords with its ringed crown, and the Eight of Swords with its ringed cage.

"Ring around the Rosy! Oh, but look at these reversals . . .

> *This Devil found her hunger*
> *in the lighter side of the half-dark corners,*
> *in the still brooding clouds of a first last night,*
> *in the Ace of Cups right space of a Knight*
> *with arms wrapped around her ribs so tight.*
> *To sleep, she keeps in balance, weighting*
> *the heavy end of a Tower's slant. Meanwhile,*
> *Hierophant gods spew a godless rant.*
> *She sees that serpentine split seam above the bored*
> *twitch of a shimmery dream when she falls*
> *into that spin asking, "who I am with me*
> *and who was I with him?"*

In Qabalah the High Priestess equates with the Virgin Mary, who wears the *Rosy* Cross, a secret society symbol. How appropriate. The High Priestess's pomegranate veil separates us from the truth. We may not have been Freemasons, but we poets and mystics spoke our own veiled language. I wasn't even sure I made sense as I released the words, but I had a general idea about the gist of it. Besides, poetry doesn't have to make sense or get the facts right. Like a good song, it just has to convey feeling. Rosy understood this. She nodded, then motioned for the waiter to get her another drink.

"You're viciously accurate, either/or."

Oh, but Rosy did not want this epiphany, and that's the problem with addiction: they go to their favorite distraction to keep from acknowledging their pain, which is considerable. Easing depression only keeps them stuck. "The way to healing is feeling," I tell my clients. And that's the last thing they want to do. They're afraid that the hurt will swallow them up, and they will never come back. The thing is, their addictions and depressions take over when we let them into our lives. This is the Devil card, in reverse.

"Gimme those cards!" Love said, snatching the deck from me. He was beyond drunk now. He was blotto.

"All right, Pandora, open the box. Read *my* cards," I challenged him. Whether Love was liquid or on dry land, whether he was trained in tarot or improvising, whether he was deemed virtuous or evil (and aren't we all both?), he would have something for me because that's just how the cards and stars and Love align. Unfailingly.

The High Priestess is a manifestation of the divine within all of us. Even within Love. (The person, not the power.) The High Priestess does not instruct anyone on anything. Her presence reminds us of what we already know inside. She wears a full moon on her headdress crown and has a crescent moon at her feet, reflecting feminine power and intuition. That night, a nearly full moon was over us in the summer desert sky, and the chic partygoers had separated themselves from our lone table, huddled close to the bar. Shaggy Love put four or five cards down haphazardly and riffed a poetic interpretation off the pictures:

"The truth goes on without you," he said.

Love then slammed down the Justice card with ridiculous force.

"It's not forgotten, just ignored by the sin living, sin livers, sin lovers. . . ."

I pondered the condition of Love's liver then and if he had considered the pun. Yeah, he was drunk. But what was he saying? It was interesting, if not clear. I felt it more than I understood it.

Next, he set down the Three of Cups, the party card, and the Four of Swords, which is depressive.

"You talk loud in crowds but go silent when alone.
Reality is separation from yourself and it approaches.
Reality leaves you breathless, so you close your eyes
to hide in the dark side."

Love said these strange words with a tone of sadness and even pity toward me. He concluded with that Devil card:

"But it's still there, without a conscience.
Reality tames you. It lacks mercy.
Everyone here is living asleep, but you, either/or.
You are dying awake."

I sat there, kind of stunned, wondering if I had heard what he had just said correctly, knowing that he was too smashed to repeat it or even understand it himself. Was he bothered by my sobriety? By my intuition? By reality? Was I?

I didn't think that I was. It shouldn't matter. None of it should matter; these were just the words of some drunk. A drunk I adored. Like any High Priestess, I listen as the soul is revealed. I empathize with his torturous inner work of turning the raw material of his suffering into something meaningful. I tend to look for signs in everything, and his truth, the truth, is that I was alone that night, even in that crowd of friends. It had been a rough few years. I was alone at home with my husband. I was alone with my family. Always alone, really. Always different from almost everyone that I hung out with. I was the black sheep. The freak. The eccentric, in my sobriety and spiritism. At my best, I liked some things about my individuality, but I also felt very much on the outside. I looked for opportunities to prove the mystics wrong; at this time in my life, I wanted to say, "No, we are not all One; we can't be because here I am, completely separate," for that is how I sometimes felt, and occasionally that notion still creeps in. I yearned to belong to the crowds that I never could be a real part of, like this one, because their despair, isolation, and separation were all too familiar. I knew that the way to nurture myself was to reach beyond myself. The way to healing is feeling, and there I was. Feeling too much, again.

I was, rather than making them responsible for their own awareness, perhaps mistakenly taking it on for them. For some reason, I loved this group of people. I think it was because I could see some of the most hurt parts of myself in them. Sometimes they even loved me back a little. In any case, it was something like love—a codependent's heaven. I kept forgetting that just my ability to read the cards negated our boundaries, our separation. It was a joke to think I was separate when I was so palpably also a part of them and their pain. Separation depends on where and how you want to look at it. When I was depressed, I dwelt in aloneness because it was familiar, the thing I knew and identified with. Peace of mind made me anxious because I had to work for it. I wasn't sure I wanted to work for anything that I couldn't count on. It is so hard to believe in what you have never known. I understood my lost friends.

I reached over gently and took the cards back from Love like a parent trying not to alarm a child teetering on a ledge or fingering a butcher knife. Now, I would read for Love. We were on a roll, and this was more of a rap battle than a tarot card reading; the cards were just props.

"You don't remember being anywhere, Fool.
Today, for you, left a long time ago.
You see limitless body counts and bitterness
through the Wands of weeks.
Now past is the was, and future is the when, and why
does The Sun card move from right above
to reverse out of your line of sight? Oh, Love!
You are alone, sinking, centered
in a Moon-dark vodka kindness.
You stay clear of what TV news is known
and absolutely here. Like radio waves, you're
transparent. Washing past the Tower's floods,
fires, and hurricanes. Almost there, you're weeping
on the edge of everything. You'll be Emperor below

the never-resting governing gulls,
despite their bird's-eye view and sharp beaks,
they forgot about love and Justice, and like this broken
Lovers' Cupid, they completely miss the point."

I spoke nonsense. Maybe. But it was fun. We enjoyed allowing the words to take us over. We always did live on the fence of reason like that, over on MySpace and there in person. To extemporize in person was just more satisfying. I think we were all a little in love with each other and with our sadness, and we were undoubtedly obsessed with words.

"Goddamnit, you're reading *me,* not the cards! I'll read the cards for myself," Love said with antagonism, grabbing them back to shuffle the deck. His spread was not so different from the one I'd just done. He threw down the Fool, the World, the Five of Swords, the Tower, and the Four of Cups.

"Ho ho ho!" he said, smacking the terrifying Tower, knowing he'd drawn his best match. But first, Love homed in the Fool's number, zero:

"I am nothing. Bad at being human. This is not a
poem; this is reality.
I lose it all a hundred times per day. I am so
irresponsible with others' feelings . . ."

Suddenly, this was not a tarot reading or a rap battle. This was a confession. The way to healing *is* feeling.

"I am a curse, a fucking coward when the truth comes.
All that's tangible is avoided.
Escape is a strategy. Through women, vodka, fighting.
The reaper is flirting, but he's too weak to hold my hand.
And so I hurt the ones who save me and destroy those
who won't."

He looked up at me. A warning?

I wanted to say, "No, Love. You are love too." But we all knew everything he said was true. The love *is* in there, but he keeps it numb.

Love continued, dizzily playing with the cards on the table, moving them in different places, right side up, upside down, and sideways as he spaced out, chanting his words from some other place.

"Existence is both defined and ended in tiny moments.
Every day we reveal our disasters.
Our thoughts are our defeat, and they fester and build like
*   ants push dirt.*
It's so easy to feed them our scraps.
It's so easy to watch them swarm.
We must quietly refuse."

I learned something valuable that night. I learned that intuition knows no bounds. Nobody has to know a thing about tarot to make it work if they are open. When Love grabbed my cards and laid them down, he had no expectations, no set understanding of traditional meanings, or interpretive symbolism. Love just went with it, and it worked.

The High Priestess is the strongest and most disciplined woman in the tarot. I never drank with them, and as of today I haven't had a drink in over thirty years. I choose not to consider it a temptation. Our thoughts are our defeat. One's charm or brilliance doesn't matter; once one begins to allow the negative thoughts and behaviors in, that dirt builds like anthills and takes us over. Today, my life, my marriage, and how I live are all so much happier than then. Looking back, I will never judge these dark and destructive darlings.

The MySpace parties turned into Facebook parties as the social network platforms evolved. It was probably next to Twitter and then to Instagram and Snapchat after that, but I quit keeping up. I choose now to love that gang from a distance. Just living is therapy, and it goes on until the end for all of us. They will make the necessary changes for survival, or they won't. They might choose numbness until their bodies give up, and then, if you think as I do, they will just have to come back and do it again. But I must quietly refuse.

Trusting Your Intuition

Trusting intuition is a hard thing for a lot of people. Heck, what am I saying? It can be challenging for me. The tarot cards secure those first intuitive senses as a pictorial back-up, but I continue to test myself and try to strengthen my intuition in different ways.

Intuitives can learn a great deal from the arts because, of course, it's basically the same thing. Consider reading some essays on writing by some of our greatest writers. They may not spell out the word *intuition*, but you will read things like, *let your character tell you where the story is going* or *listen to what your characters tell you about themselves*, and, my favorite piece of writing advice, from Robert Frost, *no surprise in the writer, no surprise in the reader*. This wisdom is all about going inside oneself and listening to intuition. Our conscious brain is too limited, too stuck in *this* world. When I write, I go to the same place I go to read tarot.

I believe that we are all intuitive to different degrees. To be alive is to be so. I am not sure that being intuitive is the same thing as being *psychic*—maybe it is. I prefer to think of intuition as heightened awareness. And we've all got some degree of ability, like singing. It's just that some people sing well, and we want to hear more, and others we beg to stop!

THE EMPRESS.

3
THE EMPRESS

The charity gala was in full swing, with long, festive tables of vegetarian and vegan food, floating bouquets of silvery balloons, and a lively jazz band. The bartenders of this swanky restaurant could hardly keep up with the demanding crowd, an assemblage dressed in their best faux fur and leather, sequins and satins. This was an event put on by an animal rights organization in St. Louis; people who dedicate their careers or pledge money and many hours of volunteer time to changing laws, rescuing strays, and helping animal causes. And they sure knew how to throw a party. The setting was an appropriate match for the Empress card, which, when she is in her element of positivity, is a card of abundance, motherhood, and creativity. She is the Pagan, the shaman, or pantheist, who finds sacredness and transcendence in animals and the natural world. The Empress manifests nature in the divine and the divine in nature. She is Mother Earth, the goddess who presides over the laws of nature. Who better than the Empress for animal causes?

The Empress embodies femininity, with her shield bearing the symbol of the goddess Venus, a circle sigil with a cross beneath as a sign of the female. Venus herself represents not only women but unity and equality with men. And while three-quarters of the people there that night were women, there were many men in attendance. The Empress wears a crown of twelve stars for the twelve signs of the zodiac and twelve tribes of Israel. All people and animals have mothers, no matter race or sexual orientation, and the Empress is a mother to all—all lives must be respected.

I donated some service hours to this event as I knew many of these attendees from my volunteer work with stray rescue groups. Over my years of service, I've learned that animal people can be the most warm-hearted, loving souls ever. But anyone who's worked with these organizations also knows that animal causes can attract many who do better with dogs and cats than with their human companions. Animal rights and rescue people often know suffering and hardship themselves, and many take abandonment, abuse, and neglect issues quite personally. Reading their tarot cards can be as heartbreaking as their rescue stories.

A woman named Joan purchased a ticket and sat down before me to have her cards read. She was perhaps a few years older than me, in her late fifties. Joan was tall and gaunt with dark, dyed hair and matching eyebrows that were a little too harsh for her sallow complexion. She had a cartoon cat tattoo on her upper left shoulder that did battle with her personality, as if to say, "See? I can be playful!" Yet her stoic presence was far too intimidating to consider such a thing.

Joan said she'd never had a tarot card reading before today; she was just doing it for the cause.

"Choose a deck," I said, motioning to my little wooden treasure chest that sat on the table, containing six different tarot decks. "The artwork in the deck you choose will work best for you."

There have been astounding matches between my clients and their decks; the illustrations they prefer reveal a lot, and often my clients tell me that cards look just like the people in their lives that they ask about too. Joan chose not to say much at all.

"You pick one," she said, not wanting to play along. I explained that it was a key part of the process for her to do it, which isn't entirely true, but I wanted her to participate. She grabbed the classic tarot, called the Universal Waite, almost in disgust. I asked her to shuffle. She cut the deck once and handed it over. Good enough.

"Do you have a question in mind or a subject you'd like me to look at, or do you just want me to see what I see?" I asked.

"Oh, I don't know," she said. This wasn't just hesitation. She had finished talking.

"OK, let's just see what I see," I said with a forced smile. The Empress on the tarot card is usually pictured as pregnant. She is pregnant with possibility, and her gown is covered with pomegranates, that many-seeded symbol again. She is happy and bright. My brightness felt false. I hate these large events, generally. Fast readings in noisy, crowded rooms are rarely going to be spiritual growth experiences. Especially when I have to yell over the noise of a live band and announcements over the PA.

I laid down Joan's cards in a seven-card triangular spread known as the Horseshoe.

"Your first card is the Empress reversed," I said. "At your core, there is a problem with mother energy. The Empress is the great creative mother, so either you struggle as a mother or struggle with your mother somehow."

Joan was stone-faced, weighing out what I'd just said. She did not comment. Maybe I hit a nerve. Or maybe she did not want to give me any hints. I understand that clients often want to see if I'm for real or just fishing. I don't want to be fishing. However, I do enjoy friendly human interaction. But this reading, of course, was not about what I wanted. My clients do not have to be friendly to have a successful reading. I pushed on.

"The next card is the Six of Cups reversed. This card reveals that you haven't let go of your past. Because it's next to the mother card, it looks like she, your mother, is the issue, and there is something you can't get over."

The Empress wears a pearl necklace, a symbol of Venus's rule over the ocean waters, the salt sea fluid that birthed all life on land. She is a physical form of the spiritual High Priestess who precedes her, and the Empress's scepter signifies her rule of the world. She is all of creation as mothers create.

There was absolute silence and still no expression from Joan.

"Your next card is the Ace of Cups reversed." I motioned to the picture of the hand outstretched with its golden chalice and flowing holy water. But upside down, as hers was, the picture looks like the hand pushes away the streams of water. Water represents love and emotion.

"You keep all your emotions in. I see everything blocked." I sure didn't need a tarot card to tell me that one.

Next I explained the Seven of Cups as a goal, which is kind of a bucket list card of her wishes and the things she wants to happen. The Seven of Wands told me how busy she would be in the next six months. Going forward, I saw a King of Wands, a congenial man, around her. But Joan didn't notice him or pick up on his interest. She would withdraw from him the same way she sat back in her chair and withdrew from me now. Her final card was the Five of Cups: mild depression and a focus on the negative.

The Empress is surrounded by wheat fields and represents fertile and cultivated soil. Sometimes she is called the Corn Goddess. Wheat and corn are more plants full of seeds, and here we were, in the Midwest, literally the farming heartland of America. Joan was busy sowing seeds of her dreams and working in her metaphorical fields, but she missed chances for happiness in her isolation and rocky soil. She did not even notice others as she plowed the ground of her days. Joan focused on what was wrong and undone and put her energy there so that she would get more and more work and problems.

"But you can do that differently, Joan. I am reading from your energy today, so this is how it will be if you continue as you have been going. We are always capable of changing things," I said.

She inhaled. "Well. I have to tell you that this reading isn't very accurate at all."

"Really?" I asked. "What feels wrong? I can add cards, and we can dig deeper to clarify anything that you—"

"I *don't* want you to add cards," she interrupted. "It doesn't fit. Nothing fits. You're talking about mother energy, and I have no kids."

"What about *your* mother?"

She stiffened, and her face grew flushed. "*My mother* died over forty years ago. I think I'd be over that by now."

The Empress is sometimes called Demeter, another Mother Earth goddess who cries for her daughter Persephone who was snatched into the underworld. In her extreme grief, Demeter plunges the world into cold and darkness, where nothing grows. Like the Empress's cycles of womanhood and fertility, the Earth cyclically falls into a winter season. Joan was stuck in an eternal winter, a reversal of the myth, as the daughter grieving for the mother.

Joan had said she lost her mother *over forty years ago*. Joan was not an old woman. This meant she had lost her mother as a teen or younger, at the time when she probably needed her the most.

"Maybe, maybe not," I said in the kindest, gentlest voice I could manage, given the fact that this woman didn't want to be talking to me any longer. "Some things we never get over, you know? And here, where it says you are keeping feelings in . . ."

"I mind my own business," she said, almost spitting out the words. I took the hint. She continued, "And I'm not a lesbian if that's what you're thinking. But there's no man. Never has been."

The Freemasons, who practiced a Catholic mysticism, see the Empress as the Blessed Virgin Mary, untouched by man and carrying the Christ who would die for man's sins. And here was Joan, both virgin and crucifix. It was interesting that Joan volunteered this information, given the fact she withheld so much else about herself. Joan grew even more rigid, if that was possible. We were both suffering through this interminable, torturous session. And yet she stayed.

"Not that you're responding to," I corrected her, trying to smile and lighten this up. "But this man is there, hanging around you somewhere, but you don't notice him."

She ignored this, the way she probably ignored this man.

"And the dreams? Whatever. Everyone has dreams. Everyone is busy," she said, before abruptly standing up. "Yes, this did not work for me. Not at all. Thank you anyway."

And with that, our reading was over.

Acceptance is another meaning of the Empress card, as Demeter had to accept that her daughter would be gone for a part of the year.

As I had to accept that some people do not want to recover.

I questioned what Joan wanted to see, if she would have liked her reading better if I had lied and told her all pleasant things. I wondered if she was ashamed of what I saw and thought I saw too much. She did not want either one of us to witness that teenage girl who lost the first person to love her. She did not want either of us to see that she never trusted enough to love anyone else ever again. It was better for her to make me wrong. If she had concluded that I was right, the grief might have been too much for her to bear. If Joan softened enough to comprehend that pain, she might be vulnerable to being hurt again. And for her, no chance at happiness was worth that risk.

Early Advice for Tarot Card Readers

It's too easy to put all your hopes and fears into your tarot card readings, so be careful. "As above, so below; as within, so without," as the Hermeticists say. Your cards reflect what's going on within. Sometimes your tarot cards will show you the things you most want—or, more frighteningly, they might reflect the things you don't want. Tarot naysayers sometimes think this is proof that tarot is a dark form of spirituality or even evil. The truth is that tarot is a mirror of the mind, a reflection of subconscious intentions and perceptions. Where is your mind? If you're very negative in thoughts and actions, negativity will appear in your tarot spread's outcomes. Best to keep the highest vibration possible, striving for love and light. If possible, strive for a mental blank slate when working with the tarot and venture in without attachment or presumption.

THE EMPEROR.

4
THE EMPEROR

I began Kate's session with a general reading using the Celtic Cross layout, and then we reviewed her work and love life in the cards. In her twenties, Kate was a pretty girl with a silver hoop piercing her right nostril, a few flowers tattooed inside her forearm, a voluptuous figure, and long dark hair. We still had about twenty minutes left before the end of the hour. The crowd at the South City St. Louis coffee shop murmured and buzzed around us as we sat at the wooden table in the far corner of their upstairs loft, where no one would interrupt us. We were already through most of our hour when she asked the question she probably had wanted to ask me first. The only question that mattered to her:

"What happened with my Dad?" She could barely speak the words.

Unlike the passive, soft, abundant mother-love of his wife and preceding card, the Empress, the Emperor is a card of masculine energy and action. He represents the father, the patriarchal system, and sometimes the military. The Emperor is a man to be respected, and he calls the shots. I think of Homer's hero Odysseus in *The Odyssey* and his famous question: *Does any person know who his father is?*

Kate reshuffled the deck, and then I put some cards down on her father. For Kate's reading, I used *The Alchemical Tarot: Renewed*, a personal favorite of mine. The brightly colored edition I like best is out of print and hard to find at a reasonable price. The Emperor in the Alchemical deck is a well-muscled, handsome man who holds an eagle on his hand, implying that he is Zeus, the mythological ruler of the gods. This deck also has the unique feature of *two* Lovers cards in its design: the artist and creator Robert Place designed a sweet, innocent version as well as a more erotic representation of love. Some tarot card readers choose their favorite version of the Lovers and put the other card back in the box. I use them both. After all, there are different kinds of love.

We turned toward the problem of her father. The sweet Lovers card landed in the center of Kate's reading, but it was in reverse, telling me that she and her father had been pulled apart. And judging from the Three of Swords next to it, that hurt. A lot.

Kate began to cry. "He was a great dad. The best. He read me stories every night and hugged me, and told me how much he loved me all the time. And then one day, he just . . . stopped. Stopped everything. He stopped loving me. I don't understand. What did I do?"

She had given this a great deal of consideration over many years. Her father had built a case of some kind against her, but she could find no clear charges and absolutely no evidence. She felt guilty, but she did not know what for.

The Emperor is not touchy-feely and may be considered cold in his single-minded approach to achieving his goals. This guy is totally in control and will not let emotion affect his judgment. He does not particularly need love or even company.

Meanwhile the few people around us in the coffee shop dwindled to a sole young man at the other end of the room, studying a textbook under a small lamp. The place was closing in half an hour and the staff came around with a big vinyl tub, collecting the dirty dishes and garbage left on tables.

Trembling, Kate said that nothing had changed in her physical, material world. She had been given all she needed and most of what she wanted. Except for the thing she wanted most: her father's love. She wiped at her eyes.

"I'm sorry. It's just . . . hard not to take it personally, you know?"

"I know. We always take things personally when we are young. How can we not, when we have only experienced a little bit of life and only as ourselves? But we have to be strong enough to tame that egocentric, childish view. If you have ever heard of *The Four Agreements,* a famous little book on finding happiness, the second agreement is 'Don't take anything personally.' Everything others do is a projection onto you of their experience. It is not about you."

Kate's Lady of Cups card in reverse told me she never broached the subject with her dad and held in all of her unhappiness. She possibly didn't want to know why. Kids don't have the emotional skills for this kind of thing. It might have felt too terrible to understand, and her fragile preadolescent self-image was not ready to confirm her greatest fear: that she was not lovable. Kate's cluelessness about the situation was there in the Fool in reverse, full of regret for never asking him. Now he had passed away and she would never again have the chance to ask him face-to-face. But there she was, a grown woman in her late twenties. She was ready to learn.

"Let's ask him directly why," I said.

I assert that we can do this in the tarot. We are all one, so Kate's energy is connected to her father's energy, regardless of whether he is living or dead. We don't have to be kept in limbo when a question this enormous controls our entire emotional lives.

"What was your father's first name?"

"Len. Short for Leonard."

"OK, Len. Tell us what happened. Why the sudden change? What killed your love?"

The Emperor wears the monarch's crown and is above all others. He wears a knight's armor under his regal dress, suggesting he is ready to join his ranks and fight at a moment's notice. I could see that Len had been fighting something. I laid down the Lady of Wands, the erotic Lovers card, and the Devil reversed.

"Oh, Kate," I gasped. "It was nothing you did. Well, what you did was . . . you grew up. How old were you when he turned cold toward you? Twelve or thirteen, I'm guessing?"

"Yes, right around then."

"Your father was watching your body change and, I think, realized that he felt physically aroused by this. He of course knew better and would not act on his feelings. He felt a lot of shame and shut down entirely to protect you."

The lights flashed, and someone from behind the counter downstairs called out, "Closing time! Please gather your things. It's time to go."

The Emperor is about power, direction, and control. He insists on his space, sets boundaries, and asserts his authority.

Whew. Never had I seen such a thing in the cards. Both of us had tears streaming down our cheeks. I put the Alchemical Tarot deck back within its cardboard box, and then put the box in my wooden tarot chest, gathered my purse, and stood up.

"I'm sorry, Kate. But your father separated from you because he loves you."

Kate and I had parked near each other outside, and so there was an awkward, silent walk together back to our cars. It was a lot for the girl to take in. What a curious world this is. What fascinating people, struggling to love and conquer their demons. And some do succeed, but there is a price.

Sometimes, the Emperor card shows up in reverse. This is an extremely difficult card, foretelling a cruel, tyrannical person or circumstance.

I once learned a tarot reading trick from a Nordic cartomancer I met in Treadwell's, an occult bookstore in London. He said that after dealing his client's cards from the top of the deck, that he always looks at the bottom card.

"This is the card that sums up the personality or the situation," he said in his consonant-heavy English with its carefully paced cadence. (What is it about accents? Foreign accents always sound more magical than our own.) After witnessing this practice in his bookstore basement reading room, I adopted this technique into my own repertoire back in the United States. There was something to this trick, and I found these bottom cards repeated for some clients. Sure enough, every time I read cards for Angela, the Emperor in reverse turned up; his meanness controlled her life either in the middle of her spread or from the bottom of the deck.

"It's a fucking cruel world," Angela said, plonking herself and a large, worn leather handbag down at our table in Blackberries, a homey yet urban café where we met for lunch.

Cruelty is what the Emperor in reverse knows and how he lives. Angela, a singer and songwriter, occasional actor, bartender, and waitress, knew everyone at the café, but then she knew almost everyone in St. Louis. She wore a knit cap and her long brown hair, full of the scent of cigarettes, was pulled to one side in a loose, messy braid. Her teeth were gray from years of smoking and her lips were so chapped it hurt me to look at them. Angela wore no makeup that morning, and still, she somehow managed to pull off a sort of "at risk yet captivating" bohemian fashion. With her youth and high cheekbones, she looked like a movie star playing the character of the ingénue in trouble.

Angela and I had a challenging relationship. She wasn't exactly a friend, because friends share a mutual interest in each other. Angela's interest was predominantly in Angela. She was the first to laughingly admit that the only place of peace in the overlapping circles of absolute narcissism and crippling self-doubt in her personal Venn diagram was that small convex center called *art*.

Angela was talented but undisciplined and reckless, justifying and romanticizing her self-destructive downward spiral into drugs and alcohol as the only life of a true artist. Her lost potential irked me, and her constant, self-inflicted drama was hard to watch. I thought of her like a kid sister or a wayward daughter for a while. Later she became a charity case. What spell had she cast upon me? How had I gotten entwined into worrying over her well-being? To use the social lingo of the day, Angela triggered me.

Angela positioned herself somewhat successfully to outsiders as a social influencer and local celebrity. Like an Emperor. But despite her friendly smile and outward presentation, and her needy appeals for my help, she was competitive and combative—also traits of the Emperor. Most of the time, Angela felt more like a *frenemy*.

"Man trouble?" I asked about Angela's "cruel world" comment.

Angela nodded. "Yeah, man trouble. Don't even get me started."

Angela had been engaged to a married man who was supposedly going to leave his wife, but after more than three years together no one needed tarot cards to see that that would never happen. She had a knack for picking the least trustworthy men, but that too was a symptom of her much larger addiction problem. She posted about this guy and others on Chasm, a private online forum where she invited me in to lurk. Angela was a leader of the Chasm girls. Their worship of Angela, her tragedies, and her glamour fed her fragile ego. The Chasm girls were kind and talented women caught up in a mess of addictions, abuse, and self-loathing. They didn't want happiness or change. They wanted tempestuous drama, frenzied excitement, and insatiable appetites. They wanted company in their misery, so they worshipped at the Cult of Angela, who gave them permission to rage and fuck up. After each and every torment a Chasm-ite posted, Angela wrote, "I'm sorry. I love you." She was the priestess offering benediction, an online temple goddess.

Initially, I felt sorry for Angela. As I was older, with more resources, I delighted in doing little things to help make her arduous life a little better: picking up the lunch tab, buying gifts or groceries, and helping with medical expenses.

Upright, the Emperor card is an organized man of vision, a powerful leader, and someone to be respected. However, when the Emperor is in reverse, he has lost his self-control and is savage and tyrannical. Sometimes he represents not so much a person but a situation or phase in life. Angela's whole life had been the Emperor in reverse, either in her vehement self-destruction or as the Emperor's victim. Women can be Emperors too, thrusting their power, direction, and control upon the world. Angela embodied the Emperor as an active go-getter, rabble-rouser, and starter of fires. Unlike most other addicts I knew, she was fiercely ambitious. Angela managed to get a lot of local music showcases and opening gigs for national touring acts. She also knew how to charm restaurant management and staff.

"The manager says I bring a little class to the place," she boasted, dabbing at her chapped lips with her napkin. And yet despite all the charm and opportunities, things rarely worked out for her.

If anyone had reason to drown her sorrows in alcohol, it was Angela. In a few short years, she lost her mother to heroin, her fiancé to a car accident, and her best friend to suicide. Angela drank to numb the hurt, complicating her life further with severe relationship, health, and money problems. Nearly everyone could see how Angela brought so much of it upon herself. Because she felt so entitled, so justified to dull the hurt, she had almost killed herself with drinking. Angela was only in her early thirties and had been hospitalized three times over that year, all brought on by her alcohol abuse. The doctors told her that she would die if she drank again, and I think she was frustrated and resentful that it hadn't happened.

Angela's attitude was anti-abundance, anti-love, anti-everything good. With the scars of her past and her current unbearably negative mindset, Angela could not and would not accept that any blessings could happen to her. She wrote herself off as "broken" and wanted to stay in that place of pity and sadness because there, she was justified in her self-loathing and destructive behavior. I had initially hoped to help Angela break this mindset. That was my mistake.

When practicing spirituality, there is this tricky balance: one must change what they can improve and keep out of the way (at the risk of looking like a heartless Emperor reversed) when others need to walk their own path. Basically, it's owning the Serenity Prayer: *God grant me the serenity to accept the things I cannot change, the courage to change the things I can, and the wisdom to know the difference.* How do we access that wisdom? I'm still trying to figure that one out.

With Angela that day, my heart felt like it was racing, and my breath was shallow. Had I ordered a decaf latte or a regular one? I'm so damned sensitive. I couldn't remember, and the viselike grip of probable caffeine did not help my serenity. The server came around again, and I asked for a glass of water.

"I believe in facing pain and being real," Angela said, playing with her food, cutting omelet pieces with her fork, and pushing them back and forth across the plate. Facing pain and being real was the whole point of the secret group: to support each other in their unhappiness, to charge into their wretchedness and claim its reality. This is actually an important thing to do. The problem with Angela and Chasm was that they lived in their pain, day in and day out. They had no plans ever to leave this semipermanent, familiar condition. As unhappy victims and martyrs, they weren't required to take responsibility for what they had screwed up, and they didn't have to fix anything, either.

"Sometimes, it *is* a cruel world," I said. "But you have to learn to look at and handle things differently, or you'll go crazy."

Originally, I thought I might be a cosponsor to Angela when she joined Alcoholics Anonymous, offering outside support. But Angela would not join AA, even when all the tarot cards revealed that it was the only way she'd successfully navigate sobriety. Like the Emperor, Angela wanted a rational, logical approach over delving into matters of messy emotion or faith. Because, of course, emotion and faith require going deep and feeling vulnerable. Deep and vulnerable is not Emperor territory.

"I don't do the God shit. Those Twelve Step groups are all about powerlessness, and I am *hella* powerful!" She raised her voice, smiled with teeth, and winked across the room at the staff behind the counter.

That afternoon, Angela was in a manic phase. The next day, she'd be calling herself a worthless piece of shit. It was always back and forth.

Angela was skilled at getting people to want to help her. She first reached out to me as a nondrinker since she was new at trying to hold it together. Like the Emperor, she needed to keep control. She also wasn't shy about showing affection, with lots of hugs and *I love you*'s, but in a bullshit kind of way, because she said this to everyone.

"I love you," Angela said to me again with a dramatic pause over her mutilated omelet. And then, she voiced what she really wanted to say. "Read my tarot cards?"

I gave her the deck to shuffle, despite knowing that she would soon argue with any advice or direction the cards gave her. She made everything hard and too much work, as most Emperors do, insisting on keeping things in their control. Angela obligatorily chatted me up first: *How's work? How are Tom and the kids?* But she did not pause or even slow to hear a reply. Then, she slumped back and embraced her favorite subject: depression.

"Except for a couple of friends and my pets, there is nothing on this planet that is worthwhile," she said. "I think I just want to die. I won't do it, not now, but I am in love with the idea of death. There is only pain in this world. Last night, I looked out my window and watched an opossum get hit by a pickup in front of my house. What timing. The second I looked out the window, wham!"

She slammed her hand on the table for effect, shaking the silverware.

"The truck kept on going, of course. *They* didn't care. I went outside, scooped it up with a shovel, and buried it."

I laid her tarot cards out while I listened to her story. Her first card was the Magician, which I applied to what she just told me.

"You're a natural-born shaman," I said. "Bless all animals you see, living and dead. That animal on the road is not in permanent darkness and abandonment. You can find peace with an animal's death by thanking it for being here and sending it back to the Great Spirit. It will return to the life force and come back again and again. You're a child of God. We all are. We all have the power to bless and move spirits on, just by being alive."

She half smiled, not really convinced or even listening, as she loaded up her next round of depression with the omelet on her fork.

"That's nice, I guess. But it's still a fucking cruel world. I mean, why is nature so bloodthirsty? While I got ready this morning, I thought I'd watch a nature show. How could I go wrong with that, ya know?"

She gave a sad, sarcastic laugh and pointed to the Ten of Swords at the top of the tarot spread. It pictures a dead body bleeding on the ground, with ten swords in its back.

"I saw a lion on TV devour a poor, kicking wildebeest alive. Ripped its throat out. And this is like, how it is *supposed* to be. We're born alone; we die alone. We are condemned to suffer under those above us in status or on the food chain."

Angela curled her fingers into air quotes and laughed again, adding, "God's plan. That's one fucking cruel God."

That Emperor, in reverse, *is* cruel. But in his positive state, he is a respected commander and revered like a god. In Greek mythology the Emperor is Zeus, who did what he wanted and didn't really care whose feelings were hurt. In Norse myth the culture of my card-reading friend in London, the Emperor is Thor. If you cross him, he throws thunder and lightning. He makes the rules. Emperors are known for ego and power, and they look down upon their underlings to help or punish them. They never view others as equals. In modern times, the Emperor may be the president of the United States or another world leader. No matter his name, right side up or upside down, the Emperor is the boss and overlord of the world's systems. But the thing is, we are all Emperors of our lives, good and bad, in what we create and project and how we view others and the world. The Emperor is our ego and the positive and negative that ego creates.

"Don't look at nature in anthropomorphic terms, Angela. Nature is a circular system, like this card, the Wheel of Fortune, also known as the Wheel of Life, that operates on instinct, without planning or emotion. When humans left the Garden of Eden for knowledge, we left that system. Humans have options, whether or not they choose to take them. That opossum wanted to cross the road, so he went for it without looking. He was hit by the Wheel of Life, or the wheel of a pickup truck, in your case."

I looked back at that Ten of Swords on the café's faux marble-topped table, casting its shadow from the top of Angela's tarot spread down onto all of her other cards. When I added a clarification card, the Emperor raised his familiar sceptered fist again.

"But let's get back to your lion on TV. Of course you know that he has to eat. That wildebeest didn't know what hit it until it was too late. Maybe it tried to get away or protect its young as an instinct for survival. Then it went into shock. It surrendered. Because it must. Instead of the permanent idea of the wildebeest dying, maybe you can think now that this wildebeest gets to *merge* its life force with the lion. I'm not talking about its dead body being digested. This is about the life force changing form to become part of the lion and enjoying the cycle of life as a new creature."

Angela took this as an opportunity to return to her favorite subject.

"*I* don't want to be a new creature. Just the same me, except with a better life. And contrary to what you or anyone else thinks, I don't want to die from drinking. That's gross. I have a spectacular, beautiful suicide planned."

I could have told her, and maybe I should have, that there is no beautiful suicide. Suicide always sucks, and it leaves anguish, ugliness, and emotional devastation behind for countless others. But there was really no telling Angela anything.

The Emperor is the center of attention in the first group of Major Arcana cards representing the worldly sequence. He sits between the mother energy of the Empress before him and the Hierophant, representing the world's institutions, in the card that follows him. In the path of the tarot, we learn that it is important to break from these worldly cards of society to find oneself.

"Angela, have you ever watched any of those ghost shows on cable TV?"

The food server came around and asked me if I wanted another latte. For reasons I didn't understand and would come to regret later that night, I said *yes*.

She laughed. "Oh God, do you take those things seriously too?"

I chuckled. "Mostly, no. But there are occasional bits of spiritual wisdom in them. One of the things I've seen is that real spiritual practitioners never speak the name of demons because that gives them power."

"So?"

"So I don't know if you know your Bible stories, but there is this one where Jesus casts a man's demons into a herd of pigs. It's the only exorcism by Jesus recorded in the Bible."

She perked up when I said *exorcism*. That's a word just dark enough to be kind of sexy to Angela. And this shadowy occult stuff, with its display of drama and ghouls, is what everyone mistakenly thinks tarot is about.

"Yeah?"

"Well, I got to thinking: Why would there even be a herd of pigs in the Middle East? Most people there are Islamic or Jewish and don't eat pork. It made no sense that they'd keep them, right? I looked it up, and sure enough, pigs need a lot of water, so they are not practical farm animals in the desert. In the Middle East, they eat chickens and goats."

"I don't get what you mean."

"Well, this just proves that this story is an allegory, not to be read literally. I reread the story more carefully. Jesus asked this demon-possessed man, 'What's your name?' He said, 'My name is Legion, for we are many.' *Legion,* of course, means a multitude. This is a lot of demons, or, more accurately, a lot of problems, right? Are you with me so far?"

"I guess."

"So, Jesus didn't say, 'OK, *Legion*. Leave this man!' He didn't give Legion the dignity of acknowledgment. Jesus straight out commanded, 'Leave this man!' and cast them into the imaginary swine. Jesus, our hypothetical role model for self-actualization, *would not name the demon.* We give power to what we name, what we focus on. Our minds are powerful and create problems, as well as solutions. Quit naming your demons, Angela. You're not only doing that, you're inviting them to move in with you."

Angela leaned back in her creaky chair, unwound the aqua-blue knitted scarf from her neck, and gave me a condescending, closed smile.

"Affirmations and all that positivity? Julia, it doesn't work. I've tried it."

Angela hadn't really tried, of course. She might have repeated some half-hearted affirmations, but the old belief systems dominated. She might have genuinely wanted some positive things, but she never believed it could be real. Hopelessness and Doubt ruled Angela's subconscious like a pair of committed lovers, till death do they part. We both knew that she liked it there, in that sad, familiar place. I could have told her it's not enough to picture yourself doing something. You have to be so into the imaginative experience that you can't see your own face because you're living it. You have to smell and taste and feel it. I could have told her nothing can be created without believing that it could happen. Yes, affirmations alone don't work. Neither does visualization by itself. Any athlete will confirm that you have to do all of that and *feel* it too. You have to know it can be possible. But Angela didn't want to hear any of this.

I returned my attention to the tarot cards on the table between our plates and silverware.

"Angela, if someone pushed you in the mud, like here on this Ten of Swords, or those trampled figures on that Death card, you'd cry. You'd say, 'Damn it! You pushed me into the mud! Fuck you!' You wouldn't stay there on the ground in the mud forever. You wouldn't wallow in it, like one of those demon-loaded pigs, and you wouldn't let it dry on you. And you're right: covering up something with a pretty dress of affirmations and positivity, like the white gown and flowers on your Strength card, will not make you beautiful, comfortable, and happy when you're caked in mud underneath. We have to acknowledge that terrible things happened, yes. Witness your Hanged Man. Witness your Death. But don't live there, and quit naming it. You have to get out of it and wash it off, like the angel of Temperance here on this card. Feel your feelings, but then release them. Do the work toward recovery. Do the therapy to let go of the pain. Don't stay in the mud, Angela. Do you follow me?"

But Angela didn't follow me or anyone. On all the social networking sites, Angela positioned herself as a thought leader, connector, and influencer, even as she looked disdainfully upon those buzzwords. She wanted to blaze the trail and have everyone follow her. Unfortunately, many of her devotees did.

"My depression is a source of my creativity," Angela said. "*The* source. I think, in a way, my depression is beautiful."

Angela didn't only name her demons; she glorified them.

Ultimately, I had to distance myself from Angela and her Chasm girls. They were just too much of a downer, and my occasional optimistic posts, meant to inspire or cheer, were ignored, challenged, or sometimes mocked. I could almost feel them saying, *Well, isn't she just a ray of fucking sunshine?* People like Angela, who don't want, or aren't brave enough to grow, won't. Not in this life, anyway. And people who think they can grow while simultaneously continuing their addictions and the blame game are kidding themselves.

However, Angela was a gift to me. She made me question my need to make her life better. I had to ask the hard questions: *How was this really about me? Was I still healing the self-destructive, self-loathing elements of my psyche? Would I ever get there?*

The Emperor's strength is his earthly dominion. He sets boundaries and owns his kingdom, and he makes the rules for his territory. He projects his thoughts into form, which is what we all do. Angela was skilled at this—we all are. It's just that her projections were tragic. Projection is a way to know where we are going; what we see outside is going on inside. Unlike his predecessor card and female companion, the Empress, the Emperor does not go into feeling. Escape of feeling is classic addiction behavior, seeking to numb emotions instead of releasing them. Angela, in this aspect, embraced more of the masculine Emperor's behavior than anything else. Despite her pretty face and forced, false *I love you*'s, Angela's energy was masculine and disconnected from emotion. While Angela thought her depression was sadness, it was an absence of emotion. Depression is another kind of numbness, a suffocation of excitement for anything.

Then I had my great epiphany. Angela explained so much for me: with her charm and talent, with her narcissism and negativity, with her general lack of interest in me or anyone else, she felt like my father, an Emperor reversed. I hadn't spoken to my father in over twenty-five years, and then he died, leaving a black hole, a *chasm,* if you will, in my life. *That* was why I was compelled to help Angela and other addicts with these behaviors. They essentially treated themselves, and me, like shit, with their sad promises of relinquishing responsibility and, one day, life itself. I had been unconsciously desperate to re-create and correct this gnawing abandonment in my psyche.

Back then, I was not enlightened enough to realize that my desire to help Angela and others like her was a red flag that my energy was all wrong. Now when I find myself drawn to someone, thinking, *Yes, your life is a mess—let me help,* I know that I have slipped into playing an Emperor's game of taking charge. Angela felt that energy from me, and she veered between needing me and battling for her independence. I sometimes forget that the other person must have their learning experiences. I sometimes forget that they are children of God as I am, fully equal, capable of living successfully if they want to take on that responsibility.

God grant me the serenity. Friends are here to teach us all kinds of heavy lessons, and they don't even have to be good friends to be successful teachers. The Emperor's ego can serve us well, like a best friend, or harm us terribly, as our worst enemy. The Emperor must determine the murky, indefinable boundaries between the lightness of pure love and charitable generosity and the darkness of enabling. That's *my* Venn diagram. And who knew? The word *venn,* in the Norse language of Norwegian, means "friend".

Where to Read the Tarot

Some people are creatures of habit and will only have successful readings in the same place, with the same rituals. Some need a candle burning. Some need quiet. Others, like me, can read in busy places like coffee shops, parties, classrooms, etc. In my experience, extroverts can take the commotion; introverts like the peace. Again, there's no right or wrong way, and you will find what works for you.

THE HIEROPHANT

5
THE HIEROPHANT

"I'm totally enlightened," the woman announced as she sat down before me at the corporate Christmas party. "So what do you have to tell me?" The room was full of people, clients, and employees of a real estate company that brought me in for their holiday celebration in an office in a strip mall.

The Hierophant lays down the law. It is the opposite of the loose, impulsive, free-wheeling Fool. The Hierophant has been through the rigors of training and has become a model of discipline. He wears a triple crown, symbolic of the three levels of rule within the church: pastor, teacher, and supreme priest.

This woman had short-cropped sandy-brown hair, perfect nails, and makeup in various shades of beige. She wore a classically tailored navy jacket over pressed slacks. Like the Catholic Church's pope, for which this card is designed, one might say that she was immaculate. For the record, *immaculate* is incredibly difficult for a tarot reader to connect with because there is an energetic block. It is a superiority complex that is somewhat antagonistic: one either has to admit defeat to them or do battle and tear them down. I like slightly messy people with vulnerabilities and mistakes and occasionally lipstick on their teeth. They're genuine, unvarnished, and their energy is more palpable.

I glanced over toward the abundant buffet table at the back of the room, where I suddenly wished I could be. People gathered around, talking and laughing, but this woman in front of me was not a part of that group for reasons I would soon understand.

"You're *totally* enlightened?" I said, hoping I'd misheard.

"Yes. I'm a psychologist. From *Harvard*. I've been through all the training. All the therapy. Freudian, Jungian, Gestalt. I have overcome all of my limitations. I know everything there is to know about myself, and today, I am a master. Now, tell me what *you* see. . . ."

I looked up at the off-white drop-panel ceiling. It was a ceiling I have seen a million times in a million other buildings. Her words were a challenge, not a question.

The Hierophant is a card of rules and requirements, dogma, and regulation. Some people live very well within these confines, so the Hierophant also reflects reward and even fame for honorable behavior.

Totally enlightened? I call bullshit. Most of us are not enlightened until we're dead. Maybe not even then; I haven't gotten there to know. Life is a journey of growing and becoming, and we are never completely there. The word *hierophant* can be broken down to *hiero,* meaning "sacred," and *phant,* a title we give a person who reveals. This woman revealed only titles and accomplishments. Enlightenment is not without passion and awe, two qualities this woman seemed to lack. But I could never know for sure because I couldn't get inside her heart. Enlightenment has moments of losing control of the ego self as we surrender to the Source, whatever we deem the Source to be. Enlightenment is a choice we strive to make, over and over, and we often screw up because we are human, after all.

I felt my pulse rise. Oh, but was this woman pushing *me* off course now? Had I slipped into a superior attitude too, to combat her? I was sucked into her game, and now we were in ego warfare and judgment of each other. It's so easy to take the bait. Escaping our egos to live in spirit is the hardest thing.

The Hierophant knows that there are many paths to enlightenment, but he prefers his own course. He also represents tradition and convention. Buddha said that someone is enlightened when they have overcome all hatred, greed, and delusion. Buddha, a true Hierophant, taught that the most enlightened people were the most humble. I hadn't talked to this woman long enough to know about hatred or greed, but I felt that she was deluded and not humble.

Sometimes the Hierophant is called "The Pope." Like the pope in opulent Vatican City, the evidence of enlightenment is not material world status and blessings like being showered in degrees, expensive clothes, art, and shiny coins. Only God can know the degree of a person's enlightenment. Other aspects of this card, reputation and approval, can't buy your soul. I couldn't tell this woman that, of course. Not at a Christmas party where her employer had generously brought me in as the entertainment. I had to smile and keep everyone happy. This was hard because as I laid down five cards for her, I could tell that the cards were powerful and not in a good way. I was supposed to keep it fun, yet I felt I was being dominated or put down.

"Can I get your first name?" I asked. The woman had controlled this reading from the moment she sat down. It wasn't comfortable for me, and there was no connection. Still, this event wasn't about *me*. I imagined how difficult it might be to be her patient. In my mind's eye, I saw her telling people what was wrong with them as she decided it. I saw her checking boxes on symptoms and rubber-stamping the names of complexes and neuroses and disorders on patients, robbing them of their humanity. But maybe this was not accurate. Maybe I needed to give her a break.

Beneath the Hierophant in the picture on the tarot card are two ministers in subordination to the pope. They attend to his needs and represent the service required by authority. Sometimes we have to sacrifice our egos for a higher purpose. In my case, that was the company writing my check.

"My name is Rachael," she stated. "*Doctor* Rachael." She sat rigidly straight in her chair, hands folded in her lap, staring me down like the Grim Reaper riding his horse in his black armor, pictured on the Death card. People lined up behind her, waiting for their own readings, and I wondered if they had any sense of the showdown happening before them.

I wanted to read Rachael's cards diplomatically and perhaps with some playfulness. To ride the fence between the positive and negative dignities these cards embodied. If I could transmute some of these symbols before us to something more, I don't know, *palatable,* maybe . . .

No, I could not. There, in front of me, I saw the illusion of the Moon, the delusion of the Seven of Cups reversed, the superficiality and ego of the Devil, the impossible-to-please Queen of Pentacles reversed, and the reputation of the Hierophant, front and center. Where was her wisdom of the Hermit, with his lantern of enlightenment? Where was her High Priestess, with her inner work? Where was her World card, showing self-actualization? No, Doctor Rachael was more interested in intimidation and impressions. Appearance, not substance, was what she was about. I wasn't even going to begin to explain these cards to her.

As a tarot reader, I want to keep it honest. But occasionally a situation arises and I am forced to conform and pretend that the cards say something that they don't. This doesn't happen a lot, and if you're wondering if I consider it unethical to do so, the answer is *Hell, yeah!* I'm still working on my own enlightenment. The thing is, I had no wisdom or information to give her because she was not open to receiving anything. A true enlightened master would have told her this calmly, keeping their integrity, even if it ruined a corporate Christmas party. Oh, but I am not there yet. I am still a slave to the world, with expectations to honor and bills to pay. On that particular evening, I tried to walk an ethical tightrope, being gently honest yet also a satisfactory entertainer.

"Rachael, tarot reflects much of the psychology you've mentioned. In fact, Carl Jung used tarot, and there is a lot of Buddhist, Jewish, and Christian symbolism informing the design of these cards. I'm sure you know already that Buddhism is a philosophy, not a religion. With the tarot, I am here to show you the path you're on. I am here to help you understand yourself and others, but you say that you have already worked all that out. I can show direction and clarify to help change things when something ahead doesn't look desirable. But if you conclude that you're already there, well, I guess there's nowhere to go."

She gave an exasperated sigh. I irritated her but, of course, the feeling was mutual.

"Will you just tell me *what path I'm on,* then?" She used my words to mock me.

"All right," I said. I heard a defensive tone in my voice—I wanted to tell Rachael a lot more than that, but I held my tongue.

I threw down some more cards to try to illuminate the path for this woman who had decided that she already had it mapped out and would not be told differently. I was a little evasive. I rambled, talking in circles; I was purposefully unclear.

"It's all a journey," I said as my fingers caressed the Fool card. "Nothing is absolutely figured out, and there is nothing we can count on. We just have to go with it and learn along the way."

She bristled. "*I* decide where I am going. I have learned all I need to, and I have done everything correctly."

Good Lord. The outwardly perfect people do often appear to be the most messed up. It's like when I see busty, Hollywoodesque blondes of a certain age who've had a lot of plastic surgery. Every one of them has had a long history of physical and emotional abuse, at least the ones who have crossed my tarot table. It's terrible to stereotype, but you get to recognize how people are when you repeatedly see these patterns.

I decided to call it quits with Rachael. She pissed me off, I annoyed her, and there was no point in continuing this session. After all, people who were actually interested in what I had to say were waiting in a growing line behind her.

"Well, Rachael, I'm sorry I didn't have much for you tonight. But I do maintain that right people come to my table to teach me lessons for my own growth too. I think I have learned something here with you. I have learned that sometimes when I perceive that it isn't right to read for someone, I should not force it, even if it's expected. I wish you well."

There are two crossed keys on the Hierophant card. These represent keys that Christ gave to St. Peter, according to Roman Catholic tradition. They show mastery of all levels of the situation, and the keys also represent the key to decoding the tarot. I have been doing this for over forty years, and I am still decoding. The same old cards present new lessons all the time.

"I see," Rachael said. "Well, I may just have to give you a negative review online. I had heard you were talented. I expected better than this."

The pope on the Hierophant card holds his right hand in the gesture of benediction. This gesture represents distinguishing what is manifest on Earth from concealed parts of the Holy Doctrine. I was not going to let a negative online review bum me out. The benediction implies that some truths are hidden in plain sight, and in a reading, getting the Hierophant card can suggest someone is in denial over details that the reader has brought to the surface.

I gave a short, forced laugh and shrugged.

"And I guess I expected an enlightened person to be a little less, oh, I don't know . . . hostile? So, there we are. Have a great evening."

I have never been very good at behaving. So much for total enlightenment. The Hierophant suggests that everything around us informs us of the truth. In reverse, he can be a rule breaker. I've always felt a kinship with that card, and I have no shame over it. I am not cut from the same Burberry cloth as Rachael. Striving for degrees and promotions in the nine-to-five world isn't my scene. I can do it, and I did it for many years. But it's not the best use of my talents, and I am miserable in that world. I am the Hierophant reversed, full-on.

"Bitch," she said under her breath as she got up and walked away from my table. Coming from her, it felt like the best compliment. The next person in line slid into Rachael's empty chair and, all smiles, held her open hands out to me, not understanding that tarot cards are different from palm readings. (I get that a lot.) I loved this new woman's sweet naiveté; she was there just to have fun.

Rachael and I had just had a battle of egos, and any participation in that war is certain death for both sides. One precept of *A Course in Miracles,* a channeled scripture that I study, is that if anyone bothers me for any reason, I must look at them with love and forgiveness. Otherwise, I carry the weight of that ugliness and harm all of humanity, especially myself. If I position myself as the Hierophant—superior, or more in the light, or if I just need to be *right*—I have jumped on the runaway ego train. And I know in my heart that anyone doing that superior attitude shtick feels less worthy than most. It's our natural response to want to take an egotist down, but we must remember to have compassion—maybe most especially to people in this place. If we seek enlightenment, we are to kill the ego and all attachment to reputation, success, and glory in the physical world. It's pretty hard to do, but that is the whole point of the crucifixion story: we die to the world in order to resurrect to a higher form.

Where to Keep Your Cards?

Keep your cards somewhere that is specially designated for them by you. I used to have a special drawer, and the only other things besides my cards were other sets of tarot decks, candles, guidebooks (for when I felt like referring to them), and some journals and pens for when I wanted to record a reading. Today I have too many decks for this one drawer so they also take up an entire bookcase.

As you read in my first chapter, some people believe you must keep cards in silk. Some people insist on a wooden box. Honestly I think that's nonsense unless you have a particular ritual that means something to you. Tarot cards will work anywhere. They are not magic. It's we who are the magic. They are merely our tools.

THE LOVERS.

6
THE LOVERS

My tarot client wanted something a little more upscale than Starbucks. I felt a little ridiculous walking into that swanky restaurant in my puffy winter jacket with my tarot card box in both hands, like I was taking up a collection for charity. My client said she preferred somewhere quiet and promised to compensate me for my extra time and travel. It felt surreal to step through the heavy glass and brass doors, leaving a ten-degree St. Louis winter windchill outside, and into a posh steakhouse that piped in cool jazz music behind palm trees in planters. It was about three in the afternoon, not lunch or dinnertime, so the eyes of all the hosts and servers rested upon me as I approached the front desk.

"I'm meeting, um"—I glanced down at my phone for the unfamiliar name—"I-fun-anya?"

The Lovers card depicts a naked Adam and Eve in the Garden of Eden, suggesting vulnerability, exposure, and innocence. In the Garden of Eden, man and woman lived purely as animals, with no egos, no knowledge, and no shame. I felt a little awkward in this fancy establishment—as if I were only wearing a fig leaf.

"Right this way, madam," said the trim young hostess, who was wearing a black shirt and slacks. She escorted me to the table of a glamorous African woman of indeterminate age. This flawless woman sat fiddling with a smartphone over an empty place setting of linen and white china.

"Hello!" the woman greeted me. She stood and shook my hand loosely. "I am Ifunanya. Call me Nani." Her accent sounded as if she'd had a British education.

"My goodness, you're beautiful!" I said aloud, unprepared for her gorgeousness. I was glad I had at least worn a dress under that bulky winter coat. Ifunanya's thin fingers felt cold and soft as I shook her delicate hand.

The Lovers may be the most alluring card in the tarot deck, and it is one of the most famous in the Major Arcana. It is colored with a glorious yellow sun over the red-winged shoulders of Archangel Uriel, one of the cherubs who presided over Adam and Eve before their expulsion from the Garden. White cumulus clouds support the angel in his holy purple robes against the backdrop of a bright blue sky. In all of my years of reading the tarot, *this* is the card that everyone wants to see. We may have concerns about health, money, or career . . . but if it came down to one question, it's love that everyone wants to know about.

"Get anything you want. My treat," Nani said. She pushed a menu across the crisp white table linen.

"I'll just have a decaf coffee," I said. For a fast and undisciplined moment, I fantasized about plowing into the warm buttered rolls the server had just put in a basket before us and maybe a crab cake sandwich and a salad, but I couldn't be doing someone's tarot reading with food in my mouth. Especially not for *this* elegant woman.

On the Lovers card, Eve gazes up toward the angel. She is equal in both position and size with her Adam. The Lovers is a card of balance and the union of opposites. Eve is not an evil temptress, despite the Bible's literal message. Many mystics, and I, do not take the Bible literally. We theorize that Adam/the man represents the conscious mind, and Eve/the woman represents the subconscious. As it takes male and female to create a child, the unity of the conscious and subconscious creates our outer lives. This is why a woman must be subservient to her husband in the Bible. It's a metaphor for the subconscious mind taking orders from the logical, rational side—yet the two are one.

Everything about Ifunanya . . . *Nani* . . . was impeccable: perfectly braided and wrapped hair, a model's figure, a striking face with smooth dark skin and high cheekbones, sparkling eyes and teeth. She was thin, tall, and exquisitely glamorous. Nani didn't wear much jewelry, save for one knockout sapphire ring on her elegant hand with its manicured red nails. There are the new millionaires and wannabes who love all the showy designer labels and attention, and then there are the more subtle, well-monied types who live in quiet elegance. Nani was one of the latter. When I looked closer, I could see she had slightly smeared black eyeliner, revealing that she had been crying.

"I have been searching for the *right* psychic," she announced, admitting that she had done her research on me: she learned of my books and even read some of the poems I had published. She combed the reviews online and saw a couple of my interviews with the local media. I knew that I would be her regular tarot card reader before I even arrived because she had felt very straightforward when we first talked on the phone. Ifunanya didn't seek party entertainment, fortune telling, or a lot of New Age platitudes. She needed someone with some actual tools to manage her life and no bullshit. I could give her that.

The angel of God rises above the Lovers on this tarot card, blessing the union. In the older decks designed by the Italians and French during the Renaissance, the Lovers card depicts the myth of a young man named Paris having to choose a partner from three goddesses. The mischievous angel Cupid sways Paris to choose Aphrodite, goddess of love, with one of his charmed arrows. The others are the more sensible women: Athena, goddess of war and power, and Hera, goddess of the Earth and wealth. Because of this old meaning, the Lovers card is often just as much about choice as it is about finding true love, and there is definitely a component of eros and sexual attraction to this card. This choice is to be safe and secure or take a risk. The Lovers card knows that we are like teenagers, weak and often not sensible when sexual abandon overtakes us. It's a wild and often vexing ride, but we love it.

"I have seen eight different psychics in the last eight days before my appointment with you," Nani said. She had dismissed them all after one session. Nani said that she was in her late forties, but she didn't look a day over thirty.

The Lovers card depicts two trees: the Tree of Knowledge of Good and Evil, positioned behind Eve, and the Tree of Life, bearing twelve flame-like fruits, behind Adam. Eve's right hand absentmindedly reaches toward the snake as it twines around her tree, a message that we can never return to innocence and the animal kingdom once we know the truth. We are exiles from the Garden because of our knowledge, not because we are evil. Sometimes, to know romantic desire feels worth giving up all the comforts of an easy life.

Nani called herself a "simple, natural girl," and so she claimed to be embarrassed to tote around her black mink coat with her, but it had been a fierce Midwestern winter, and she was used to a warmer climate. She dropped a few morsels about her life: she was born in Nigeria to a prominent family and studied at M.I.T. She met Steve Jobs while traveling in India, studying Zen, and found herself working at a creative little start-up called Apple. She bought stock and held on to it until she became a multimillionaire, retiring at her husband's request in her thirties. She had three homes: one in Paris, one near her family in Abuja, and one where we were, in St. Louis, to have a place with an international airport and first-class living in the middle of it all. I was surprised she didn't choose Chicago or New York, or maybe Rio or Tokyo, above St. Louis. I soon learned that Ifunanya was full of surprises and that she had the fortitude and the money to do whatever she wanted.

I asked Nani what she wanted to know. Was there a decision I could help her with? Was she seeking her path to enlightenment or trying to help others? I sensed she was stuck in limbo. This woman with everything still lacked peace of mind.

The Lovers card's lure is incompleteness, the idea that we can't be whole without another person and that we are not fully actualized alone, which is ridiculous. We would never look at a newborn baby, a perfect soul, and say they needed a lover to be fully human. There is always inadequacy, impossibility, and imperfection around the idea of romantic love. All romantic love has a shadow side, and the ancient myths clarified that romance did not necessarily have anything to do with sensible marriage arrangements.

"Tell me what you see around my love life," she directed, choosing the black-and-white Hermetic tarot deck from my box as the one that would best speak for her. Some people see this deck as frightening, with its lack of color. Others see it as direct. My male clients tend to choose this deck more than the women. "It's a black-and-white world; I want black-and-white answers," Nani said.

When a married person asks about their love life, I know there is usually a cause for concern. I laid the cards down and soon saw that Nani's life was full of drama: there was the King of Cups, the Lovers, and the Devil, all in reverse. She confided then that her marriage of twenty-one years had never been consummated. The Two of Cups showed that her husband, Frederick, is her best friend, but his Moon in reverse and that Devil card again revealed that he had a very dark side. With added cards and Nani's comments, I learned that he had a taste for S&M, suffered from STDs, and had a propensity for sexual binges, occasionally with men. Despite this, Nani had been faithful to him for many years until she met a man in St. Louis. That man was a sexy and fun King of Wands who had just died, judging by the terrible Ten of Swords.

"In my bed," she said, patting at her shining dark eyes with a tissue.

On the Lovers card, Adam and Eve's hands are open, receptive to influence from above. The angel represents God's help and can signify that assistance may come from unexpected sources. And yet we remember that Eve's right hand nearly touches that serpent. There is ever the potential for our subconscious to turn toward temptation. And love? That's the ultimate temptation, right? Like the exile from the Garden, love has a relationship with death. When love shows up, it says, *Your old life is over, and you'll never be the same.*

The Hierophant card revealed that Nani's St. Louis lover was also married. The Page of Swords reversed showed a scandal about her attending his funeral and the subsequent difficulties communicating with his grown children and family friends. This was a Ten of Cups reversed funeral ceremony: everyone was upside down and in so much grief. Nani was in self-torment, feeling guilty because she was the Other Woman, and even guiltier for wanting to be loved.

The cumulus clouds on the Lovers card suggest that through an initial attraction, something takes form. The result is either love or a lack of love, depending on if the card is right side up or upside down. The Lovers, therefore, can be the greatest joy or suffering. I have found that, directly or indirectly, every problem my clients have ultimately comes down to being an issue of love. The spiritual doctrine *A Course in Miracles* says that there are only two things in all creation: Love and Fear. And Fear does not exist.

I sat with Nani in the restaurant for three hours.

"You are frighteningly honest," she told me. "It's a little scary. But that is just what I need right now."

Ifunanya was not the first to tell me that. Some people are uncomfortable with my directness and even my own vulnerability and personal sharing. I want them to know we are all one, and they are not alone.

"I have been there," I said, "In that place where I had so much shame and pain because all I wanted was to be loved, yet I did not feel that I deserved love. I knew it in my head but not in my heart. I have sought love in the wrong places and with the wrong people too. So many of us have, although most don't talk about it. You are not alone in this."

My vulnerability is my greatest strength. In this work, anyway.

If you look at the equality meaning of the Lovers card, then the cure to problems of love *is* love. But true love begins with the self, and that's an old trope that is the last thing a hurting person wants to hear. They want to search outside themselves for a quick fix, so they find facsimiles of love and love-like experiences that tend to be impossible to resist and then come tearing apart, hurting all the more.

"How much do I owe you?" Nani asked when it was all over. She had already bought me coffee and offered to buy me a carry-out lunch and dinner, which I declined. She paid me more than double my rate in cash.

"I hope this will be enough? Let's work again soon." She handed me a generous handful of twenty-dollar bills, artfully folded so that I could count them in groups of hundreds.

After that, I saw Ifunanya in spurts and phases. She had manic periods where she was infatuated or broken-hearted by men usually far beneath her social status; she fell for the firefighters, the fishermen, and the dance instructors, who all took her gifts, money, and body when she let them. She fell for narcissists, users, and abusers. I soon learned that it was Nani's standard practice to pay everyone double or even triple their rates, and she seemed to seek out those who took advantage, insulted her, or disregarded her feelings. I vowed to myself to never abuse her generosity, and when I doubled my rates a year later I did not tell her, knowing she would still overpay me in any case. Perhaps I was a fool because I knew that she could surely afford it, but I could not be one of *those* people in her life. I was always well compensated by Nani.

Ifunanya's readings were invariably and unfailingly about men. Of course. She did everything to assist her lovers and would-be lovers, to better their lives and give them what they needed for their success. They rarely considered her happiness in return, or else they did it in that narcissistic mode of occasional "love bombs" of homemade cards and gifts, but nothing consistent enough that she could count on it or feel secure. Nani was often alone, feigning strength and hiding her bitterness and melancholy behind a glamorous exterior. Through occasional treats from her lovers, like a drug that sometimes gets you high but mostly just keeps you steady, Nani was addicted to love. She was starved for love. But why did she perpetually seek the darkest and most evil men to give it to her?

The Biblical character of Adam, on the Lovers card, was formed out of the mud of the Earth. As Adam is our forefather, we are all soiled—children of dirt, risen and molded by God from the slime and muck of the world.

"Tell me about your father, Nani," I asked her so many times. Nani usually responded with a brief statement about his success, his irreproachable character, and that he was an influential, well-respected man. He was practically a king in Nigeria and possibly more powerful.

It didn't make a lot of sense to me. A heterosexual woman's father generally imprints upon her what a man's love looks like, and she will spend the rest of her unconscious life either seeking to duplicate it if it was happy or correct it if it was deficient. When I laid down Nani's cards, her father was at the heart of her Celtic Cross spread on every occasion but forever upside down, causing inconsolable torment that she carried into her life every day. Across our many readings, had I misread these mean and broken kings somehow? Continuously?

"It keeps coming back to your father," I said again with a shrug. "All of the wicked men in your life are revealed to be an echo of him." By the time of this reading, Nani had been my client for more than four years. But now Nani's aging mother had fallen ill, and in this weak moment she revealed the key.

"Please don't tell me anything you see around my mother," she requested, changing the subject. "I couldn't take it. My mummy is the most important person in my life. When I was a toddler, my father beat me almost to death. A few times. After the last event, Mummy took me away to protect me and gave up her very prosperous life to ensure my safety."

Now it all made sense.

I adored Nani then. I have since continued to work with her and coach her toward seeing how her father subconsciously called the shots in her love life. It was easier for Nani to look at his darkness after he passed. Or it may have been more challenging, as she had great battles with family in executing his complicated estate. I think leaving her that mess was his last attempt to hurt her. But she got through it all and discovered her strength, and I pray one day that she will find a love that doesn't have to hurt so badly.

Our parents are our first models of authority, so they set the tone for what God *feels* like. If we do not feel that our parents had our best interests in mind for love, safety, or happiness, we probably will struggle to believe in a God that wants the best for us. We get broken perceptions of love from this struggle. How can we see love in our lives if we don't fully believe in it? And so many of us, like Nani, have a subconscious theme controlling everything that says we are only safe when we do not allow ourselves to be loved.

In the Book of Genesis, the story of Adam and Eve begins with them falling asleep in the Garden of Eden. The exile of man and woman is all a dream. The entirety of our lives is an illusion. Nowhere in the Book of Genesis, or anywhere else in the Bible, does it state that Adam and Eve ever awoke from that dream. When will we awake? When we are in love, we want to stay asleep forever.

Learning the Basics

Get one or more good books that help you define the cards and learn the fundamental spreads. Go to your local bookstore and thumb through some until you find one that appeals to you. The right ones will tell you that they are meant for you. Then read the introductions, look up cards, and practice the spreads. When you sense you've got a handle on the fundamentals, put the books back on the bookshelf and trust yourself. I first learned from the now out-of-print *Understanding the Tarot* by Jane Lyle.

THE CHARIOT.

7
THE CHARIOT

From the outside Ryan appeared to know how to live well. He was a tall, athletic, good-looking guy who had been a regular tarot client for years. Ryan dressed in expensive clothes, drove a new Lexus, and worked in public relations. When he called me for a reading, I expected the usual: to take a look at his love life and his work, and maybe check on his money situation. I met a girlfriend of his once, and he had also brought me into his home to meet and read for his relatives. By this reading, he and I felt like family after so many years of working together. We met in a restaurant this time, and Ryan said he had something different for me that day.

"I want you to look at someone named Jim and tell me what you see."

The Chariot is a card of drive and ambition, symbolizing the mind directing the actions of life. It is generally considered an excellent card, signifying victory and success. Some say the Chariot driver is the god Ares, victorious at war. The ancient Greeks also told of Hades, who kidnapped Persephone in a golden chariot to take her to the underworld. The Chariot is about success in the superficial and physical world. This single-minded ambition often forgets about the soul.

I never ask my clients questions, except for the first name of the person they are asking about. If I were to inquire into the details of a relationship, I might be accused of leading the client to give me information. And so I keep to the cards on the table, relying on sheer intuition, and seeing what presents itself.

"Ugh. Jim does not look to be in a good place," I said. "This Ten of Swords is a painful ending. Followed by the Four of Swords reversed . . . oh, that's bad. I mean, sometimes that's even physical death. Certainly, it's depression and darkness. Inner *and* outer darkness. Page of Swords reversed shows some kind of lie. And there is a Queen of Cups in reverse—his mother? I am getting that it's his mother—she is upset. Does that make sense to you?"

Ryan's expression grew serious.

"More than you know," he nodded. He began to explain. "Jim is dead. You nailed that. Can you add cards and tell me more about the lie and his mother?"

I did. Under the card about the lie, I turned over the Chariot in reverse. The Chariot represents all kinds of journeying, physical and spiritual, and the emotions accompanying it: absence, wandering, longing, separation, chaos, and adventure.

"The Chariot is an interesting card," I said. "It's a card of winning when it's right side up. But Jim's Chariot is upside down. When this happens, what we call being in reverse, it means failure or loss. It warns about misusing power, excessive pride, and arrogance. But it can also be about traveling, the chariot as a vehicle. My sense with Jim is that both meanings, failure and loss, and representing an actual vehicle, should be considered."

Ryan marveled. He looked around, almost for a witness or a television crew to jump out and declare he was being punked.

"Yeah, it's both meanings, Julia. All of it. The Chariot is a physical car and a death. A car crash. Can you go on?"

Next I clarified that reversed Page of Swords and Queen with the Justice card. (Clarifying in tarot is to pull another card to look deeper into the meaning of the cards already on the table.)

I said, "I think someone lied to his mother, and Jim wants to make it right."

The color drained from Ryan's face.

"That makes sense," he said. "So here's the thing: my friend Jim had a pretty serious drinking problem as a young person. But he went into the military and got cleaned up. He was out with some friends of ours—I wasn't there—and they all got drunk. They piled into a car, and this other guy was driving. They wrecked the car, and Jim died."

"Oh God, how awful." I gasped.

"Jim wasn't driving. The guys freaked out, of course. The driver would have gone to jail for manslaughter, you know? He would have lost everything he had worked so hard for. The guys decided to move the body and make it look like Jim had been the driver. They decided that Jim would have wanted it that way."

Both of us suppressed tears. Ryan's eyes shone from the recognition of carrying this painful secret and losing his friend. My eyes brimmed from the shock of this reading. I felt that Ryan was perhaps a little too fervent in describing the details of this story to have not been there himself, as he said, but I kept that to myself.

The Chariot focuses on a single goal or value. His problem is that he then closes himself off to all other possibilities. He lives solely in the world, and he is more concerned about his reputation and success than what is truly meaningful.

"Oh my God . . ." Ryan continued. "It's the mom part that's so sad. His mom believed that her son screwed up again, and he died because of it. But you're telling me that Jim wants his mom to know the truth."

"Yes, he does. Ryan. You weren't there for sure, right?"

He gave a vigorous nod. "No way. I wouldn't have done that."

I hoped that he told the truth.

"Maybe you could make it right? Maybe you could tip the mother off and let her handle it however she might want to?"

"Maybe," he said.

Maybe, I thought. *But I doubt it.*

The Chariot's number is seven, considered a number of the

moon, which completes a quarter of its monthly cycle every seven days. The Chariot, therefore, is a card also to mark the passage of time.

I never asked Ryan about it again. This was the kind of reading I didn't know how to process. I respect client confidentiality, but what to do about the crime of manslaughter? *I* can't report anything. I don't have any last names, dates, or even a place where this happened. I can hardly tell the police that I saw it in tarot cards. They'd laugh me out of the station.

The Chariot card is interesting as the vehicle in the picture appears to have no wheels. This is likely because wheels connote change in the tarot. Perhaps the Chariot doesn't know how to roll with what life gives him, and so everything is a drag, or he must force everything. Ryan perceived life like this: behind his exemplary looks, all the glitz, and his impressive material possessions were the pressures of a mountain of debt, the fear of not finding his true love, and, of course, pervading guilt over his friend Jim. Ryan was feeling at least a low-level depression most of the time. He lost track of what was important and wasn't in the driver's seat of his own life.

There are feminine aspects on the Chariot card that are also interesting to note: the vehicle bears a shield in the traditional shape of the yoni, symbolizing female genitals. The black and white sphinxes who lead this chariot are endowed with large maternal breasts. The driver holds invisible reins on these sphinxes, who are said to represent the feminine subconscious that leads him. That nagging mama is eternally in the back of our minds, trying to keep us on the right path. She can be gentle, and she can be fierce.

I was no angel in my youth and went off-track for a while myself. Ryan and I survived it, and Jim did not. Sometimes we abduct ourselves for that wild ride, but not everyone has the maturity and discipline to slow down . . . or the confidence to insist upon a designated driver.

Interpreting Symbolism

Take time living with each card, especially the Major Arcana cards. Carry a single card around with you for a day. Study it. Look at all the different codes and patterns within the picture. Realize that colors mean something. That new shapes seem to emerge or shapes you had previously noticed now change perspective. That it's all metaphor and symbolism. Read the definition of the card and find those meanings represented within the picture. This is how the meanings will stay with you.

8
JUSTICE

> Author's note: In early tarot decks, the Justice card was number eight in the Major Arcana. The modern turn-of-the-century decks switched this card with Strength, originally number eleven. Justice and Strength are thought to be similar: one aspect assists the other. Medieval beliefs associated heavenly rewards and retribution with the number eight, and the number eight on its side is the infinity sign associated with karma. I keep to the traditional ordering, so despite the number eleven on the card's picture, you are reading Justice here as number eight, in its rightful place.

Theo smiled when I took the tarot cards out of my bag and set them on the table in his art studio.

"Oh, yes. I was hoping you'd bring those. I want to understand what these things are about. I want to get a close look at the illustrations too. Who knows? Maybe something from them will find its way into my next painting."

It wasn't hard to imagine tarot in Theo's art. His modern art sensibilities incorporated everyday objects infused with an abundance of symbolism and weirdness: embryos with bolts in them, fish on land, faces blending into landscape, and landscape forming faces.

Theo's liver-spotted hands shook as he held the cards, giving each one a careful look through the thick, fingerprinted 1970s-style glasses perched on his nose. I tried not to look down at his right foot, swollen and gangrenous from diabetes. He kept it wrapped in gauze and perched on a stool while he awaited surgery to amputate his dying toes. Once a handsome guy (he had made sure that I had seen old pictures of him), Theo now looked every bit of his ninety years. What a life he'd had! Running all over Europe, studying with the masters, romancing the women. He'd won international art awards, including a Guggenheim. He'd served in World War II, where he painted camouflage on tanks in Normandy. He loved to tell the story about the fake tanks they painted on plywood to expand the visual threat of the Allied attack. Theo wrote poetry and published some books, but mostly he painted.

Justice is said to be the tarot card for gifts from the gods, like art and poetry, which some possess and some do not. It isn't fair that only some of us should be so blessed, is it?

"Here's a picture for you," he said, handing me a sketch of a face with a third eye entitled "The Visionary." He had had it mounted and ready to be framed.

"I'm honored!" I said, giving him a tight hug. He was the father I never had and always wanted. I tried to come to see him at least once a week. I did not charge for Theo's readings. It was a gift to me just to spend time with him; a signed picture was a bonus. I placed the drawing down carefully and took the tarot cards from his hands to lay them out.

"How much can you see with those things?" he pressed.

"Oh, I usually start with a little past, present, and future," I said, falling into my spiel. "I am showing you what you already know on a higher subconscious level, and I mirror it back to you."

"Can you see something that somebody does not want to reveal?"

"Sometimes," I laughed. "But I don't cross lines. I'll respect your privacy, and I wouldn't mention anything I saw if it were not helpful to you."

"But what if someone is, you know, not a good person? Can you see that?"

The Justice card features an androgynous-looking judge whom many ascribe to be the Greek goddess Athena. In one hand she holds a sword of severity and in the other, the scales of balance. This tarot Justice, however, is not blindfolded. She sees everything that's going on.

I looked Theo straight in the eyes and smiled. "Everyone I meet is a good person, more or less. We all screw up sometimes. I don't judge," I told him. "None of us can judge."

"Could you see, I don't know . . . a murderer?"

What a strange thing to ask. I wondered if Theo carried some horrible memories of the war. Probably that was it. He was a very old man. Perhaps he hadn't been thinking clearly or used the wrong words. The Justice card can also reflect one's intellectual equilibrium.

Theo's cards went down on the table in the great wheel of the Celtic Cross. At his core was the Three of Swords, a great deal of emotional woe and heartache, crossed by a Page of Cups: child energy.

I was a little confused, knowing Theo and knowing that his daughter was older than me. No children or grandchildren complicated his life, as far as I could tell. But it's not for me to figure things out. I just report.

"It's David," he said in a whisper. "My son. Who passed . . ."

"I'm sorry, Theo. I didn't know."

"He was born with Down's syndrome. Died when he was thirty."

Theo elaborated on all the cards of imagination and creativity that showed up around David: the Seven of Cups, the Empress. It was as if Theo knew their meanings without me saying a word.

"He was so gifted! Such imagination!" he exclaimed. Theo was lost in a melancholy reverie then, excited about his son's artistic ability and his clever mind, despite his mental disability.

"Retardation, they called it back then in the fifties. But David's mind was not retarded. Maybe his body was, but not his mind. He was brilliant! Brilliant and simple and kind."

Theo took off his glasses to wipe away a tear.

In Theo's cards I next saw Temperance in reverse. I explained that this was health gone awry or not being strong enough to fight something.

"That's right. People don't understand that with Down's syndrome, it's not just how the faces look and the fat tongues. It's the whole insides. The organs are not in the right place. They don't live long because of *that*."

"There's the Justice in reverse card, Theo. I guess what we're reading is that it's a crime. The whole situation is unjust. Wrong. This is all so terribly sad."

"A crime . . ." Theo said quietly. "Yes. A crime. But I couldn't help it. . . ."

"Of course, you couldn't do anything," I offered, trying to soothe him. "It's just one of those things. Life is not fair."

Theo appeared even more shaken and upset. Oh Lord, the last thing I wanted to do was kill an old man with my tarot cards!

Theo tapped a paint-stained fingernail onto the Ace of Swords reversed, reading the cards himself now. "Those goddamn doctors! They made David their guinea pig! Cutting into him all the time. Everything was going wrong, and they kept giving the kid surgery. Surgery on top of surgery! I had no say in the matter as his father! How was I supposed to explain what was happening to him when he had the brain of a six-year-old? How was I supposed to explain the torture?"

Justice bears the sword of severity. Athena can really be a bitch.

I set the cards down and held his shaky hand.

"Julia, I am an evil person. I am a bad man. But I couldn't do it. I couldn't watch my boy suffer anymore. . . ."

Was Theo saying what I thought he was saying?

"Theo," I said, "You don't have to tell. . . ."

I wasn't ready to hear any more. But he kept on talking in barely a whisper.

"I did what any one of us would have wanted. It wasn't right for the doctors to do that to him. It wasn't right, goddamnit. We were alone in the hospital, so I kissed David goodbye and took his pillow . . . It wasn't right."

The scales of Justice show that balance will prevail. The solution to an issue may not be what was wanted or expected, but it is best for all parties. Justice is impartial, and decisions are made without emotion. The question is, what happens when spiritual justice does not adhere to the world's word of law?

I never pressed for details. I don't know how Theo got away with it, how there would not have been questions. Perhaps David was so infirm that no one had expected him to live anyway. When I got home from seeing Theo, I thought about pulling a card for David. I wondered if David felt that he was murdered or if he recognized this as his father's act of love. I decided it was none of my business. It is right and just that I do not know.

Relying on Intuition vs. Reading the Books

So . . . you've mastered the Celtic Cross, maybe the Horseshoe spread, and some other primary layouts that you've learned in your books. How do you start becoming independent from the books to rely solely on your intuition?

First off, stop being afraid to be wrong. The biggest enemy of intuition is being afraid to be wrong. Our egos are the problem. Learn the meat-and-potatoes for the suits and their corresponding numerology. Get familiar with the Major Arcana. And then let the pictures tell you more.

That said, I still check into books now and then. Especially when I'm reading for myself. The reason is that I am often too biased and too concerned about my outcome to give myself accurate readings. I taught my best friend how to read so that I could have an objective perspective and get out of my own way. If it's a subject with an outcome you're ambivalent about, that's a different story. Then, your intuition should be just fine.

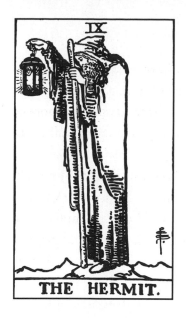

THE HERMIT.

9
THE HERMIT

Before I learned how to protect myself energetically, wedding receptions used to make me physically ill. More than a few times, after working a reception, I pulled over on the side of the road and threw up before I even got home. You would think a wedding would be all happiness, but the truth is that they are roller coasters of emotion. There is happiness, yes. But while everyone smiles at the bride and groom taking their vows, it's a mix of energies in the crowd: The guy full of addictions is taking advantage of the open bar. The lonely, recently widowed woman is trying to smile. There is the woman in the sexy red dress looking for love (isn't there *always* that woman in the red dress?). Children run through the partygoers, overloaded with sugar from rainbow-colored macarons, chasing bubbles and having temper tantrums. The partygoers watch the ceremony and question their own lives inside their heads. They wonder if they made the right or the wrong choice for their own spouses. Some are so moved with happiness, yet they wish that dearly departed Mom could have been there to see it. Others doubt love entirely and smirk inside, placing bets on how long the couple will last before the divorce. Some witness the seeming happiness around them, yet they are saddened by the love they lost or never had. It all comes out in their tarot cards.

The setup was ideal. The reception was held on the grounds of St. Louis's Forest Park on an early summer day, and they had erected a glittery little tent to shade me from the sun and offer cover if it rained. Inside was a pretty little table and some chairs. I sat and read cards to a steadily growing line of attendees. I have to keep things moving at these prodigious events, so I do quick five card spreads.

When the Hermit card falls right side up, he is the wise man in the tarot. He may choose to be with someone or not, but he is not needy. He lives simply and is unencumbered by the trappings of the world. While he looks old and frail, his mind and heart are strong.

An older man sat down in my tent. His skin was as gray as the few hairs left on his head.

"Hi," I said. "What's your name?" There is information even in just a name and how they say it. The tone of their voices tells me *bully* or *victim, saint* or *sinner.* My work will be more challenging if I don't get a name.

"Harold," the man said.

The Hermit is on a quest for enlightenment. He stands atop a mountain with his lantern to guide others. He is a spiritual leader who has exiled himself from the world, as Jesus went into the desert and Buddha journeyed alone with nothing. In reverse, the Hermit is another thing entirely. Being alone, in this case, is a problem. Sometimes, the Hermit needs alone time and can't get it. Sometimes he is terrified of being alone. Sometimes he can't escape being alone. Always, there is a reason that the Hermit is alone, and if he looks inward he will discover the answer.

I asked Harold to shuffle the cards, and I laid the solemn spread down, one by one: the Empress, reversed; the Three of Swords; the Page of Cups reversed; the Hierophant reversed; the Four of Swords. The bride walked past our tent in her long white gown, peeking in and offering us glasses of champagne. We both declined.

I don't always get the tarot cards' message immediately. I talk it through to the person I'm reading for. Sometimes these scary and strange symbols make sense to me, and sometimes they do not. The questioner almost always understands my subtle musings and outrageous declarations because they know their lives better than I do. I just speak what I see.

"To have an Empress as a first card is almost always about your mother because our mother is the first person we meet on this life journey and your first model of what love looks like. But yours is reversed, so there is sorrow there."

Harold flinched but said nothing. I knew that I had hit the core issue.

"The Three of Swords is a lot of emotional despair, and the Page of Cups reversed tells me that you kept it all in, never told anyone. Oh, no! That you never expressed any love. . . ."

Harold wiped at a tear.

"The Hierophant is often a marriage card, but that's reversed too. It either never happened, or it didn't work out for you. And so here you are, Harold . . . isolated and alone . . . that's the Four of Swords, here. You present yourself as the Hermit, but oh, there is an awful lot of heartache. Harold, you were never loved, and you never knew how to *do* love. You have never known it. . . ."

He began to weep openly. I was glad for the tent walls so that the partygoers outside could not see. I reached across the cards and placed my hand on his.

"I'm so very sorry this happened to you." I was full of emotion. Sometimes I get pulled right into the experience, which can be pretty powerful. "But here you are, still alive. You can still love, even now. You just have to dare to allow it, and you never did. It never felt safe, but the thing is, love isn't supposed to feel safe. We have to risk it. But there is still time. Life goes by pretty fast, huh?"

The Hermit is an elder, with his walking stick that connects him to the earth and symbolizes his inner strength. His hooded cloak represents spiritual protection and a shield from the outside world. He is a strange and quiet card to introduce the lively and glittery Wheel of Fortune, which comes next in the tarot's Major Arcana. He is about retreating alone and readying for the next stage in life.

Harold gave a small smile. I don't think he said a single word to me after his name, but his actions told me I was on the right path.

"Harold, when we're hurt, we build walls to protect ourselves. Those walls can be pretty good at keeping out the distress. Unfortunately, they also keep out all closeness and intimacy. If you're here on this planet, alive and breathing, that means you still have learning to do. And we are here to learn love in all its forms: family, romantic, friendship, community, nation, and world. That's it. Love is the whole reason we exist. So you might as well get the lesson now and finish your life in a happy place than have to come back and do it all again." Harold stared hard into my eyes with a look that agreed with me. He nodded his head *yes*.

The Hermit is said to correspond with the solitary god Saturn and the melancholy mood, which was held to be an essential path to creative inspiration and self-knowledge. He removes himself from the world's stimulus, and on his spiritual retreat he gathers strength in his silence. Some Hermits do this for a day, forty days, or decades. There is no wrong process to growing. Our higher selves guide us where we need to go.

While most of the partygoers I had seen before him had been second-guessing their perfectly good mates, Harold was a decent and kind man who had never had even a mediocre mate. Some can be choosy about companionship, while others starve for it.

Harold was still crying when he gathered both of my hands in his and whispered, "Thank you." Kool and the Gang's over-played hit, "Celebration," had just ended. The line to visit my tent had disappeared, as everyone at the wedding now crowded around someone giving a speech near the dance floor. The microphone buzzed and gave some feedback as the deejay made introductions. Harold wiped his face with a white cotton handkerchief, the kind only older men still carry, and he walked back toward the party, dissolving into the crowd.

I think about him often and wonder, was he ever brave enough to take down his walls and step into the world?

How Many Tarot Card Layouts (Spreads) Do You Need to Know?

You need to know right now that you can create your own layouts. You don't have to memorize a hundred different spreads. When I first began doing the Celtic Cross spread (a practical, all-encompassing spread that I suggest everyone learn), I sometimes had an especially intriguing card where I wanted to know more. In that case, I'd lay a "clarification" card over the top of it—the next card in the deck. Sometimes I'd do several clarifications. Trust that the order doesn't matter and that the right cards will settle where needed.

Sometimes the clarification makes you want to dig more deeply into that aspect. You can do "mini-crosses" inside the Celtic Cross. Just lay an overhead past, present, and future around the card of intrigue, and you can often get a clear picture of what's going on there.

I know one tarot card reader who doesn't use layouts at all. He tosses the cards into messy piles and reads what comes to him. Trust that however you do it will be the right way for you.

WHEEL of FORTUNE.

10
THE WHEEL OF
FORTUNE

Shu-Ling was a striking, impeccably dressed Taiwanese immigrant I had been seeing as a client for a couple of years. In keeping with current fashion, she dyed her natural jet-black hair with a mix of orange and firehouse red. She had been in the United States for ten years and had become an American citizen, but now she was on the fence about whether to return to Taiwan. Like some of my other immigrant clients, it was hard for her to make friends in the United States. Shu-Ling had had an American boyfriend for about six months, but that didn't last. When she found me as her tarot card reader a year earlier, he had just dumped her. It was sometimes a struggle to understand her English, so relying on my intuition was most important.

When I first met Shu-Ling, she told me she was forty-five years old, which was also my age at the time. "Ah, I am forty-five too—1963. The year of the Rabbit," I said, referencing the Chinese zodiac, which she was sure to know. There was, of course, a hair's chance (or *hare's* chance) that she had been born in the Year of the Tiger, which covered the early part of 1963, but I thought I'd risk it. Shu-Ling laughed. She was indeed born in the Year of the Rabbit. This was not mysticism, just connection.

"Chinese here don't like me," she explained, "because I from rich family. They have hard to make life in America. They think I have only easy." And so Shu-Ling was ignored by her people, who had also immigrated here to this midwestern town on the other side of the world.

The Wheel of Fortune is also sometimes called the Wheel of Life. The Wheel just keeps turning, like time itself, and so this tarot card can be used to read on the subject of time. The Wheel of Fortune bears alchemical symbols for the four elements, earth, air, fire, and water, and cherubim, and may also be considered the Wheel of the Zodiac.

This card also shares the ideas of forward movement and materialism with the Chariot, although the Wheel symbol maintains balance. The Wheel of Fortune is the last card in the Major Arcana to represent the outer world's stages, trials, and rewards. The tarot cards that follow the Wheel represent the second stage of initiation into the spiritual world, *dissolution,* when the false self is broken down. Some people never leave the first stage.

This particular night was one of my tougher sessions with Shu-Ling. I knew something was wrong as she was normally so pulled together. But this time, she met me at our usual Starbucks somewhat in disguise. She was wearing no makeup and had on a baseball cap and glasses. She wore a sweatsuit over her tiny frame and kept her ski jacket on the entire time. Of course, even her sweatsuit and ski jacket were more elegant than anything I had, but it startled me to see her without the pressed neat dress, matching designer bag, and shoes. Shu-Ling's fingernails were still flawlessly manicured.

"Merry Christmas!" Shu-Ling said, overly brightly, and handed me a Macy's gift card. Very sweet. Once we got to talking, however, Shu-Ling whispered everything. She had been having a rough holiday season.

When my clients see the Wheel of Fortune in reverse, their expressions often drop. "Does this mean bad luck?" they ask.

I tell them, "The Taoists say, 'Good luck, bad luck, there is no luck. It just *is.*' You make the best of it, and the Wheel keeps on turning. And Buddha says there is a gift in everything if you want to look for it. Sometimes it's harder to find than other times."

Shu-Ling worked as an art teacher in an inner-city public school.

She loved her kids and had a great zeal for the work, although she expressed exasperation because the parents and other teachers did nothing for their children. Shu-Ling even bought the kids food so that they would have enough energy for class. She couldn't get them to stay focused and work. The kids, of course, just wanted to hang out. She felt like her talents were wasted in her job, but that was not her real problem.

For as long as I had known Shu-Ling, the Wheel of Fortune reversed (loss of fortune), and the Devil reversed (addiction) dominated her tarot readings, as well as the Five of Pentacles, a card of poverty. Over and over, these cards reared up and announced their presence. Shu-Ling had so much shame around these subjects. She practically read the cards herself.

"Casino," Shu-Ling whispered. I wasn't surprised. The Wheel of Fortune looks like a roulette wheel. Shu-Ling told me that she borrowed $100,000 from family and friends to pay debts from gambling last year. *One hundred thousand.* Had I heard that right? I hoped that I had gotten something wrong in her translation. I worked with her throughout that time, understanding that she was alone, depressed, and suffering from addiction issues, but I was not sure of the details. I knew it was bad, but I didn't know how bad. I learned a little more each time I saw her. Now Shu-Ling was in trouble again.

Several cards indicate change in the tarot: the High Priestess is about inner and unseen change. Death is a transformative change, and the Tower is a sudden change. The Wheel of Fortune is a change of position from what came before. If things have been going well, it is a warning. If things have been troublesome, the Wheel of Fortune brings hope.

"I lose big yesterday," Shu-Ling whispered to me.

I never asked how much. I never asked anything because, as the tarot card reader, I was supposed to be the one to give information. Shu-Ling was a textbook gambling addict, and she wasn't at all cognizant of the fact. She believed in magical thinking and luck, and she may have sought me as a tarot card reader to support these beliefs.

She was quite mistaken. Now, she thought spiritual forces conspired against her.

"I come in with the wish, and I have it, but all the wish is broke," she said with tears in her eyes. There was a childlike sweetness in her use of English, but there was nothing sweet about her problem. Gambling addiction is as destructive as any other addiction I've witnessed, and the suffering is terrible.

Some people look at the Wheel of Fortune as a card foretelling that the divine will intercede in the affairs of man. It suggests that God is above chance. However, most tarot readers acknowledge that two figures on the Wheel, the serpent and the Devil, hang out on the lower half. The center of the Wheel is a point of unity and perfect balance as circumstances continue to turn and change.

I told Shu-Ling that I was unsure whether I had understood her accurately, and she tried again.

"All the machines keep going and going, you know? Eating my money. They keep going, and I win little bit, but I lost lot. I say, 'What am I doing here?' And then, I got a wish. Julia, I get easily five hundred, three hundred, with no problem. 'I can win,' I tell myself. Five hundred dollar. Four thousand dollar. Six thousand dollar. I can do it. I do all the time! I keep going. Say, 'I want the money back. A little bit.' The more I go, the more I lose. Out of control, like you say. Just like you tell me. Like heroin, like you tell me."

Over the first couple of years that I worked with Shu-Ling, I begged her to get help. But she still thought she might be able to manage this, and as long as she believed that, I knew her trouble would continue. Her reasoning was a struggle to understand when looking from the outside:

"What do I do?" she cried. "I try to change my GPS on my drive to take me a different road, but it send me back to Highway 94!" This highway crossed the river, where some of our St. Louis–area casinos are. She had to cross the river to get home. "Then I get light that gas low. I have to pull over on exit by casino!"

"And so you went in," I said, finishing her story. I knew that grandiose casino entrance and its expansive adjoining parking lot. So many people. So much noise. It is an absolute nightmare to go in, as far as I'm concerned. There was nothing convenient about the long drive to a six-floor parking garage and then elevators into the casino. Creepy people, cigarette smoke, sweaty desperation, and too many drunks, in my opinion.

"Yes. I had to! And Julia," Shu-Ling whispered, even quieter, "I had two jackpot, five thousand and six thousand. I went to get my check, and ATM was broke! I couldn't deposit, only bring back. I lost it all. And lot more."

Positioned on top of the Wheel of Fortune is a blue sphinx holding a sword like the sphinxes on the Chariot card, this symbolizes equilibrium in perpetual motion. It is so easy to become confused with everything buzzing and turning and ringing. I did understand that spellbound dream of walking into all those lights and sounds the first time I experienced it. It is sort of like being a kid at your first carnival or amusement park, except that the casino is a place of no time, no daylight, no parents, play money, and nothing feels real.

Shu-Ling said there were no casinos in Taiwan, only games like cards and mah-jongg on special state-sanctioned days. When her father came to America to visit, going to the casino was always his favorite thing.

"My daddy has Devil card too," she said.

But Daddy can afford it.

"Shu-Ling, you *have* to stop going. Please understand this. It will destroy you."

"It just that casino always so nice. People smile and bring me good drinks and food. Everything so pretty and happy there. Always! It not bad there. It bad *after*. When I am there, I am not so alone."

Oh, it was heartbreaking. A week earlier, I read cards for a Mexican immigrant who also talked of her loneliness, sitting in the same Starbucks seat Shu-Ling sat in now. It is not easy to be out of one's culture, far from all family and friends. Shu-Ling had just been looking for something to assuage her sadness. Overhead, the Christmas carols blared: *Just hear those sleigh bells jingling a ding-dong ding-a-ling!* I wished I could turn it off.

"Shu-Ling, have you heard of that 1-800-BETS-OFF number?"

She nodded. She wasn't quite ready to do that. She told me about all the great trips she got from the casino chains. They flew her west to Vegas or down to Tunica and put her up in resplendent hotels with free meals. I explained that they were not free; she was paying for them. Nothing is free. That casinos are a business whose purpose is to make money, not give it away.

"Shu-Ling, you agree that this is like a drug for you. Just like some people use heroin. You can't do just a little gambling. A person can't do just a little heroin. You are going to have to stop entirely or it will destroy you. Do you understand this?"

The Wheel of Fortune bears the number ten, the end of a cycle and a new beginning. The Wheel is about setting circumstances in motion, the laws of cause and effect associated with Eastern karma, and the idea of "As you sow, so you shall reap."

Shu-Ling nodded again but with a look of uncertainty. I took out my phone and looked up Gambler's Anonymous on Google. I sent her the link. "Look, there's a meeting in West County. If you feel too alone, call me. I'll go with you."

Like I had time for that. But the girl needed a friend. I stopped charging her a while back. I couldn't take her money anymore in good conscience. She tried to compensate me by offering to take me on a trip to Las Vegas, all expenses paid, with her casino points. It was a trip I had to decline.

"I have last question," she said, motioning toward the cards again. "Will casino pay me back?"

For a second, I thought that she was asking if the casino might be compassionate and refund her money. No, Shu-Ling was still talking about luck. I put some cards down. I don't even remember what they were, but I barely looked at them.

"No, Shu-Ling. The casino is not going to pay you back."

Anyone could have foreseen that.

Shu-Ling gave a sad sigh. "Nobody with me, you know what I mean? I with myself. I have no children. I have one failed marriage. Many things going wrong with me." And then she pulled the strap of her designer bag over her shoulder and stood up to leave.

Boundaries are so hard, and there is no balance hanging on to the Wheel's edge. Try as we might, we can't steer the Wheel of Fortune. I wished I could have been the friend Shu-Ling needed, but I am married with a family, a busy career, and a different life. We walked outside to head to our vehicles, and I hugged her goodbye. As I drove away, I saw her in her still-parked car. She sat, sobbing into her hands, hunched over her steering wheel. I wondered if I would hear from her again soon, if she would ask me to escort her one day to a Gambler's Anonymous meeting instead of to Vegas. I predicted that I would not. It was really too bad about that. Her luck was running out.

Reading the Cards for Simple Answers

Sometimes all you need is one card for a yes or no question. But know that the tarot is seldom that simple, and there are many shades of gray in an answer. Some readers will interpret a straight-up card as a yes and a reversed card as a no. Sometimes this works, but I believe that it is too limiting and lends no interpretation. You might just as easily flip a coin for something that simple. However, if I ask a question like *Will I ever get this book published?* my answer may be, for example, a Queen of Pentacles, straight up. That would be a definite *yes* because pentacles are around material wealth and success. However, in reverse, there can be problems with money, greed, etc. There would be a negative aspect to that success, emotionally and financially, if the success were achieved. But maybe the card I picked was a Five of Wands. Well, fives are a struggle, but Wands are creative. So I'd say *yes* again, only with a struggle and perhaps a long wait. But what if it's in reverse? Well, that's defeat, so that answer would be *no*. You see . . . your answer is mainly in the symbolism of the card you pick and what your intuition tells you that it means.

11
STRENGTH

It took forever to head south to that remote country home, away from everything I knew so well in the St. Louis metropolitan area. To top it off, I had to track road signs as the location was unfindable by my GPS when I exited the highway. I had heard of Ironton, and there it was, an old Missouri mining town designated as the county seat in 1857. Ironton was rather lovely in its thick forests and abandoned quarries and pockets of decrepitude. Ironton's blue-hued hills contain a courthouse, a school, a library, and a post office. Outside of the farms and homes around it, it was an easy highway exit to miss, a blip of development in the vast countryside.

The Strength card in the modern tarot decks bears the Roman numeral VIII, but like my car's GPS, this card is off in its positioning in the tarot's Major Arcana, where it was once numeral XI before the Golden Dawn changed it. I keep Strength in its original position of card number eleven. Like Ironton, Missouri, the Strength card's picture features a landscape of country green meadows, trees, and a picturesque blue mountain.

I wasn't working in a country shanty, however. Toting my box of magic, I was welcomed into a sprawling split-level home with a pool, tennis court, and professional landscaping. This was a group of about fifteen women, a bachelorette party the night before a wedding, but fortunately, without the drinking games, condom crowns, and penis swizzle sticks—I've worked plenty of those too. This party was more relaxed and family friendly.

They brought me into a little back room with wood paneling that served as a sewing room and a place to bunk overflow guests. Framed needlepoint and vintage Coca-Cola ads from the turn of the century decorated the walls.

Gina walked in first to get a reading. She had long, dark hair that hung in her face. She wore no makeup and hid from the world, unnoticed in plain sight.

I had her shuffle the cards, and I laid them out one by one, in what is known as a Horseshoe spread, to show where Gina was now, what was working, what she knew, what her conflict was, what she didn't know, her best advice, and the outcome she should expect on the course she was on.

I explained that her beginning card, the Seven of Swords reversed, is interpreted as a card of exploitation.

"I'm a rape victim," Gina told me straight out. "I want to know if I will ever recover completely."

It was then that I noticed that Gina still protected her body from the world and from any chance of being attractive, keeping herself wrapped in a cloak and long ivory dress, despite it being a hot summer evening. Next I pulled out the Strength card.

The Strength card features a graceful young woman in a flowing white gown, taming a lion. She soothes the angry beast not with brutality but with love and the power of her character. In reverse, she may not understand that she possesses this strength. No one who gets the Strength card, right side up or reversed, can't overcome their problems.

I had to stop and breathe for a moment, letting the confusion and dolor settle inside me. Because I have been there and have seen other clients go through rape too. I have seen some clients numb out and destroy their bodies in a kind of self-loathing with drugs, alcohol, or food, and I was glad Gina hadn't gone there. Gina needed to give herself permission to express the misery and anger over it to release it so that it would stop controlling her, but she had shut down all feelings out of shock.

"I have forgotten how to live, and I am unable to trust enough to even go on a date," the woman, who was in her thirties, confessed.

I am not trained as a counselor or therapist, yet this work calls me to step into those roles. It's emotionally exhausting, and it frightens me a little how much my clients put their trust in me. I just have to trust God that I will channel the right advice. When things get very heavy, I always suggest they rage privately, journal extensively, and get professional help. I let Spirit direct my answers, but I have faith in science. I focus on listening and loving people through whatever they're going through and doing the right thing. It works well enough.

"Please, honey, get counseling," I said. "This isn't a quick-fix thing. You will have to do some hard emotional work, getting through all the tangled feelings you probably don't want to look at. But by acknowledging and releasing your hurt and anger, you will get the control back in your life."

Gina thanked me with a hug. She seemed ready to begin. She was strong enough.

Janice came in next. She was a heavy-set, plain-spoken, no-nonsense, middle-aged woman. Her Ten of Wands reversed revealed that she carried the load of everything: all the work, all the chores, the kids and grandkids, and pets. Their country home, the Ten of Pentacles in reverse, had fields to tend, and a recent flood had damaged their property. She had hired help for all of it, but she didn't have the money. She worked at the local bank, the only job for miles. Janice's cards revealed that she was married to a disabled man, who showed up as the King of Cups in reverse. With the Moon card, which often reveals an illness, I could tell that she was also not doing well physically or emotionally.

"I don't know how much longer I can keep this up," she said. "Some days, I look at my husband, and even though I love him, I *hate* him! I can't abandon him because he could not survive without me and has no one else. I made my vows."

Janice wept through her anger, letting it all out. "But he's not the man I married. All he does is eat and watch TV. He doesn't even care that I have given all my life to serving him. And for what? For what!? I'm not appreciated. I'm not loved. I just want to escape."

The Strength card is about conquering our animal nature: the lust, rage, and other instincts dominating us and keeping us out of balance. When we do not rely upon inner spiritual strength, character, and discipline, we usually have many regrets, guilt, and sometimes punishment.

"I am so, so sorry this is happening to you, Janice." We sat quietly for a long minute, the sounds of the party washing over us.

"Janice, is there a way you can feel compassion for him? Because loving him, despite him being an unappreciative ass, is your road to healing. When we hold anger or blame against another, it is also against ourselves because we are all one energetically. You don't have to like who he is today or what he is doing. You don't have to like a damned thing about the whole situation. But can you look deep into your heart and understand that maybe this TV and eating he is doing is his depression? Maybe there is a lot of withdrawal because he isn't sharing what has become of him? Try to find a way to love him, and it will lighten your load, at least a little bit."

Janice took a tissue and dabbed her eyes, nodding. She didn't hate who he used to be; she hated what he had become. She knew deep down that he probably hated himself too.

I turned over the Strength card.

"I believe that there is a higher purpose for all events and people in our lives. But I know that is too hard to consider when you're in so much grief. Let's talk about you right now. Not your husband, not your problems, just you. What in your life is still functioning, Janice? What can you still be grateful for? You have to find it. For your own sanity. The things we focus on are the things that grow, and the current situation is not working too well for you."

"That's for sure," she laughed.

"Janice, I promise you, there is not a war-torn refugee out there who wouldn't give anything to have your worst day. So, let's tally it up. You *do* have blessings. You still have a place to live. You have food and warmth in the winter and shade in the summer. Your roof keeps the rain off, even if it leaks in your basement. You, as decision-maker and the sole earner, call the shots. Janice, I am not dismissing your problems; they are absolutely real and hurtful. Your pain is coming off you in waves, and I don't know how to fix it. But I want you to start practicing to grow the good. Build your gratitude for what you can so that more favorable things can happen. It will give you the strength and clarity you need to decide for yourself how to change things. And only you can change things. Not me, and not any advice I have. But you have to change something because you're going to crack if you stay on the course you're on."

The Strength card has been defined as "unviolated innocence" by Arthur Waite, the modern tarot deck creator. The female character of Strength subdues the lion with acts of charity and kindness, expecting nothing in return.

I worked through the rest of the party crowd, some giddy and drunk, some troubled, some serious. They moved through one by one, hanging their dirty laundry before me, revealing all the ways they kept themselves stuck in their problems: There was the peppery divorcée who called her ex a "was-band," with a laugh, but she was clearly still smarting. There were the young women desperately seeking love and passion or trying to force it in their current relationships. There was the alcoholic with her many reasons to continue her consumption and the destructive thrill of drinking. I handled them all with spiritual firmness about taking responsibility for one's own life because nobody else is going to do it. That is not always the answer they want to hear.

The Strength card is sometimes called "Lust" in the Victorian *enthusiasm and vigor* senses of the word, and it is also known as "Fortitude," implying courage. However defined, Strength is what is needed for transformation from pain to something better.

Finally, the woman who owned the house sat down before me. She was the mother of the bride, a weary, gray-haired woman with deep crinkles around her eyes like a pie crust indented with a fork. I liked her on the spot.

"What's your name?" I asked. As I've said before, there is something in a person's name. There is a whole pseudo-science based on names called *nomenology,* which I think is mostly nonsense. But I do appreciate that a name resonates with a kind of spirit. My name, Julia, means *young,* and I think it fits. I'll never totally grow up, and I am fine with that.

"Mary," she said. There was a conquered kind of ache in her voice—like she had walked barefoot into Hell's fire and spat in the Devil's face. Her cards reflected this.

The luxury of her country home was no substitute for happiness. Mary's Judgement* in reverse showed that someone made a negative decision against her, and Justice in reverse showed it to be unfair. The Knight of Swords reversed told me that she had had a falling out with one of her sons, a significant betrayal. The Page of Cups reversed, the Four of Swords, and the Hanged Man told me that her son had kept her grandchildren from her for a long time out of revenge.

In medieval times the image of a virgin taming a beast, like on the Strength card, was an artistic echo of goddess ancestors such as Artemis, the Ancient Greek huntress, or her Roman counterpart, Diana. The Strength card is about pacifying our base, animal natures. Revenge is one of the lower spiritual vibrations from which there is no benefit. Nothing good can happen with revenge, and revenge won't fix anything for either party.

"Years," Mary cried, confirming everything. "They're here tonight, my grandkids. We have been reunited, but it has been hard, and I don't know if they remember me enough to still love me. I don't know what they know."

I wept too, processing her distress at having lost those precious years of watching kids grow up, in the agony of being at odds with one's son. This is very similar to parental alienation, which is a narcissistic game of control that can be incredibly destructive to families.

When I put down the cards for Mary, I saw the kids all in their

---

*The British spelling is used in the Rider-Waite Tarot deck.

different ages and stages of self-absorption. The teens liked being back, but they hadn't really considered the loss, other than remembering that Grandma's house was fun in the summertime. Their Grandma loved them deeply, but as kids are inclined to do, they didn't think much about giving it back. It was the youngest girl who showed up in the cards, the sweet Page of Cups, who took it very personally.

"That's my Emma," Mary said. "She's almost thirteen."

I reached across the table and held Mary's hands, and I said that I hoped this reading would help give her some peace, even though I could not take the suffering away.

"Before you go, would you read for the kids?" she asked. I said sure.

I read for the oldest girl first, who at sixteen was more interested in her friends and boyfriends and was lying to cover up some unapproved-of antics. It was all there with her Devil card, and the Seven of Swords and the Page of Wands reversed. She blushed, and I laughed. I spoke to her about karma and how adolescence is the time to practice being an adult.

Next was her thirteen-year-old sister, Emma. Emma was awkward and shy, with long curly blonde hair pulled back in a ponytail. She straddled her chair, not fully committing to sitting down. She played with a glass of water she had carried in, rubbing a finger up and down over beads of condensation on the side. As I put her cards down, I explained that I saw a woman who loved her very much in her past, a Queen of Cups. Emma's eyes welled up. I saw the Judgement card and said, "You're very smart!"

There was something about this comment that reduced the sweet girl to tears.

"Can you tell me more about that woman?" she asked in a small voice.

I told her that this Queen was either a mother or grandmother. I could see it clicking with Emma. I knew her story before she came in, but I did not have to mention that to keep it honest. The cards did most of the talking as the girl took in the pictures. Her next card was the Eight of Swords, the lady in the cage.

"She has been sealed away, and you couldn't get to her," I said, elaborating on what she did or did not already know. I told her that the Knight of Swords reversed shows that there had been a lie told to the girl about this woman and that Emma had been betrayed. And then I saw the love energy of the Strength card and reuniting, and I said, "You can tell this woman anything. She loves you, she always has, and she always will."

The girl fell apart. We both stood up, and I hugged her. She sobbed and sobbed into my shirt. When she gathered herself, she left the room. Beyond the door, I heard someone ask, "Emma, have you been crying?"

The woman on the Strength card has the lemniscate, or infinity symbol, over her head. She turns her attention to divine matters, and her great efforts are for the long term, not just today. Because she seeks a balance of power, echoes of the Justice card are in her meaning. This is why the positions of Strength and Justice were switched in the modern tarot.

I don't know how the evening went after my readings finished, but the energy in the room seemed noticeably happier as I departed. Mary, the bride's mother, tipped me generously and hugged me. I got into my car and drove down the dark country road, my headlights punching through the blackness of dense trees. Silver moonlight washed through twisted branches, and I thought to myself, "I think I fixed something."

Cards as Talismans

Some cards will become very special to you. Let them. I slept with the Strength card under my pillow for a year during my divorce. Superstitious? Maybe. It wasn't that I believed the card could do anything for me. It's that I wanted to dwell on the concept of it and have the vibrations of the idea stay with me in my unconscious.

THE HANGED MAN.

12
THE HANGED MAN

Jay was in a panic, even on that quiet, sunny day outside the art museum.

"Sometimes I forget how to breathe," he said as he tried to inhale deeply and then found himself caught between a swallow and a gasp.

"I begin to think about how I appear, how the world sees me, and I can't do something as simple as walking across the street."

Panic attacks. I had known Jay for over a decade, since he was a kid. He is the son of my friend Carol. A couple of years back, I taught him how to read tarot cards and he was a natural. Sometimes he read for me while I gave him pointers. Now he was a young adult, and I watched him slowly unravel on this particular afternoon. His mother blamed herself. And Jay blamed himself—for everything wrong, all the time, to annoying degrees that sounded like excuses for not changing anything. Maybe he never was all that stable. As we all watched this boy struggle to become a man, we worried about him.

The Hanged Man card pictures a young man hanging by his foot from the gallows. It would be miserable to be in this upside-down position, but he is strangely content with a placid expression. He is waiting for a great awakening. Like the Hierophant card, the Hanged Man has a connection with the divine. The Hierophant reaches the divine through the outer world of religion and society, while the Hanged Man reaches it through inner, mystical experience.

Jay and I went to the St. Louis Art Museum just to hang out. He pulled out the old deck of tarot cards I had given him. The cardboard box they originally came in was long gone. The cards were battered, faded, and held together with a rubber band.

"Put down some cards for me?" Jay asked, already shuffling and about to hand them over.

We sat outside in the sunshine on a flat marble bench that could have been the same one pictured on the Two of Swords card. There was no wind on this spring day in Forest Park. No wind is a blessing for tarot card readers outside, but no wind felt like a metaphor for Jay's lack of breath. His first card, the card at his core in the Celtic Cross spread I laid out for him, was the Hanged Man.

The Hanged Man is sometimes called the Scapegoat or the Martyr, and he is said to suffer for others' sins. His body makes an upside-down number four, the four elements of the Earth. This four is kind of a contradiction to the four of the Emperor, the man who has his shit together.

"You overthink everything," I told him. "The Hanged Man hangs from his foot, not his neck. You are not dying. You are simply putting all this weight and pressure and meaning on things that don't matter, and it keeps you stuck in limbo. He sees everything upside down, and so do you. Jay, no one cares about these things but you. When was the last time you looked at someone and judged how *they* breathe or walk across the street?"

He shrugged. My words rained on him lightly. Soon they evaporated and were forgotten. Then it was back to gasping. Qabalah says that depression, addiction, and anxiety are brought on by travails we don't want to accept. Jay repressed deep pain, and it all came out in panic. He needed a doctor or a counselor, but he rejected that path because they just wanted to medicate him. I hated medication as a first option, but it might have been appropriate for Jay.

The card that represented Jay's face to the world was, not surprisingly, the Empress. She is his true love, creativity. At his best, Jay was an artist and a musician. When he was ten, I watched him surge from one single-minded obsession to the next as I'd never seen. Jay didn't just play guitar, for instance. He played guitar constantly, carrying it everywhere, learning every popular new song. Jay couldn't have been more than twelve when he got invited to play on stage with professional bands at concerts. He was so cool back then, with his curly shoulder-length hair, skinny little body, and earnest facial expressions as he felt his way through the rhythms with intuitive grace. To integrate music into your being like that at such a young age—that stuff can't be taught. He was a musical prodigy. We were all so sure of it.

But Jay had a crossing card, which is an obstacle. It was the Moon, and that's a formidable one to override. The Moon in reverse has a dark side, and it is in a different place in the sky every day. It never settles down. Something shifted inside Jay a couple of years later, and the guitar lost its shine. He still picked it up to play now and then, but his next phase was to become physical, in sports. Perhaps it was a hormonal thing. The Moon card can represent hormones too. His mother and I crossed our fingers and prayed that the guitar would return eventually. Lord knows she spent enough on his lessons. Still, one couldn't knock him for biking, skateboarding, basketball, and inline skates. All this movement was represented by the Chariot in reverse in his tarot card reading. That Chariot reversed fell in the position of his recent past. Wheels, you see. Jay had a desire to move ahead, but it was out of control. Jay had no direction.

Inline skates were pretty innocuous as a passion. But in Jay's hands—or on his feet, in this case—no passion was safe. Jay decided that the skates must become *a part of him*. He resolved to live on the wheels so that they were a personal expression like that Hanged Man picture that shows him forever tied to his tree. Carol humored him and figured he'd grow tired of it. For a summer, we watched him shoot hoops, grocery shop, and even sleep in his skates. Did he bathe or change his socks? I don't know. I could never forget the day I stood with them both in line to enter a music festival at Riverport Amphitheater. The security guard looked down at Jay's feet.

"He can't wear those in here," the guard said, giving us a look that followed with, *So get the kid back to the car and get him some shoes.* You know. Like normal people.

"It's all he has!" Carol moaned as if this guy should discern that for himself. She scolded the guard. "You don't understand. *He doesn't wear shoes.*" And that's how Jay is, was, and probably always will be, even grown-up in his twenties. He didn't play by the rules of society, and he couldn't understand why that should bother anybody.

The guard looked at them both incredulously. There was no reasoning with Carol or her son; they were removed from normal societal thought. With the throng of thousands pressing in from behind them in line, the guard sighed and waved us all in.

I remembered all of these sweet and funny stories about him. Jay had been such a gift to me. But Jay was not the one to walk down memory lane with on this particular afternoon. Now, Jay was ruled by panic attacks. The word *panic* derives its meaning from possession by the wild nature god Pan. Pan is the only god of the Ancient Greeks who actually dies. The Hanged Man is continually in a stage of dying but never dead. Both archetypes fit Jay.

As Jay grew up, he became a friend and someone to practice spiritual exercises with. We had some successful attempts at mind reading, him sending messages and mental pictures and me receiving them, often in precise detail. Everything was about words and pictures with us, and we were very in sync. Jay explored magic with me within the visual arts, and he was the one I called when I saw my name, *Julia Gordon,* in a photo of Beethoven's "Immortal Beloved" letters, written in the great composer's hand. Jay was also the one to whom I could say, "Look! There is my name, *Julie,* what my family calls me, written in the Hanged Man's tunic. Maybe that is why so much of my life has been in limbo."

Jay would see these things and acknowledge that he thought they were spiritual signs of something significant for me. Of what, we weren't sure. But something.

The Hanged Man is usually interpreted as life in suspension or limbo. Sometimes, he is read as someone who has a big decision to make. When he is in reverse, he procrastinates and does not want to make a decision. And so, he stays stuck. And with that placid expression on his face, he doesn't seem to care.

Jay was more than competent at everything he put his mind to, but the art! He was wonderful! A natural sense of proportion. A brain that could capture the absurd, rein it in, and make it say something meaningful. Art shows began to recognize him. The Chicago Art Institute awarded him a summer scholarship. It all looked so promising. What happened?

"Joy is for life. Sadness is for art," Jay said to me as if that explained everything.

The Hanged Man is a card of consequences. We must pay for our sins. In some depictions of the Hanged Man, coins fall from his pockets. Money is not important where the Hanged Man is going, and it never mattered much to Jay.

I kept on with Jay's tarot card reading. At the top of the spread was the Tower reversed.

"Whew, Jay. You've got to get rid of this self-destructive energy. It's showing up as your *personal goal*. I love you, and you drive me absolutely crazy, you know. I can't help you. Only you can get your shit together."

When Jay was sixteen, he attempted suicide shortly after dropping out of high school. He had also self-sabotaged the art institute opportunity, getting kicked out for refusing to adhere to a curfew. The next thing we knew, he downed a bottle of ibuprofen with whiskey. His mother found him in time, unconscious in his vomit, and got him to the hospital to have his stomach pumped. After all that happened, I cried and cried. Jay, my boy. Almost my boy, in any case. As the Hanged Man is headed, Jay was also on his descent to the Underworld. The Hanged Man precedes tarot card number thirteen: Death.

Jay and I spent a lot of time together after that. Then Jay went to Green Bay, Wisconsin, for a while to live with an aunt and finish high school. That didn't work out, either. He ended up living with junkies and wrote me delightfully weird letters teetering back and forth between depression and mania. He came home prematurely balding, bearded, looking and behaving like a young Vincent Van Gogh.

The Seven of Cups card was in the position for Jay's near future. It's a card of dreams, the bucket list, and everything you want to happen.

The trouble with this card is that they're just these images floating in the air, and the figure in the front can't quite reach the dreams without taking some definitive action.

"You've got to make these dreams happen," I said. "Put dates on the calendar, save up, start moving things in that direction."

Art became an active part of his ADD, as his mother said. Jay sketched on notebooks, table surfaces, walls. Almost unconsciously. He never did anything without paper and pen around. He stopped painting because he became too exasperated with not being able to create the fantastic things in his mind. Nothing was ever good enough, and so he attempted nothing. Nothing at all but dreams.

Jay's future cards were mixed. The Eight of Wands told me what I already knew, that job offers and opportunities came his way often, but the Ace of Wands reversed revealed that he never got around to following through. The Five of Pentacles wasn't shy about the fact that he was intermittently homeless and lived off the kindness of strangers, myself included. Jay was terrified half the time about where he was going and what would happen to him next, yet he made no effort to create change. And so Jay's reading ended with the Death card reversed, stuck in this hellish place. He passively watched the world pummel the shit out of him as if he were his own science experiment. His mother continued to blame herself, like that could fix anything.

"I'm such a failure. I'm a failure as a mother," Carol said whenever the subject of her eldest son came up.

I told her she wasn't. I mean, look at him. He was there, still alive. He was healthy. He had a kind heart. Maybe the best heart. He knew she loved him.

"You have not failed him," I said again.

But now, in this reading outdoors on a windless day, the two of us anchored on a museum bench, I was more of a mother than a tarot card reader for Jay.

"A couple of weeks ago, you told me you were looking into working at that summer camp. They wanted you! It must be too late for that now. And you were talking about going back to school or training to teach English in Asia. *Any one of those things* could have been great for you. What happened?"

"They all seemed good at the moment. But . . ." Jay trailed off. "It's just that I can't be sure about any of them. I don't want to make a stupid mistake."

It was back to that Hanged Man. Jay couldn't make a decision. He waited and waited for enlightenment, for that halo around the Hanged Man's head. And like the card's mythology, Jay took on the role of the martyr and the victim. The Hanged Man is Prometheus, the ancient Greek god who sacrifices himself to give humanity fire. And oh boy, do the other gods make Prometheus pay for that disobedience. Jay had all of Prometheus's rebellious attitude and suffering, only with none of the accomplishments.

Jay turned the tarot card reading into a joke.

"All right, Julia . . . I let you look inside my soul. Now, I own you," he cackled, reaching toward me like a wicked witch. At least he was smiling again.

I wasn't going to drop it. This was Jay's life we were talking about. I was so conflicted, wanting to push him to get it right, hating having to witness him on his path. I wanted to read for him and love and support him, but not direct his life. Yet I gave him the lecture I wished I could hold inside. It is so hard being human.

"Who is sure about anything?" I told Jay. "You just have to try stuff—to see what sticks. You have to live. You're not living at all. Do you see that? I mean, here you are, one of the brightest and most talented guys I know, virtually homeless, working a part-time job, scooping ice cream. . . ."

A week earlier, I had dropped in unexpectedly to see him in that ice cream parlor. He was determined to hold on to his favorite aspects of childhood, a pleasing trait, except that he maintained zero responsibility and couldn't support himself. As he dipped into a vat of mint chocolate chip and put it in a cup for me, he looked amazed and dreamy and said, "It's so weird to see you in this place. People like you almost never come in here."

"Is that a good thing or a bad thing?"

"It's a shame," he said, and then he came around from the counter and hugged me. He can be so sweet when he's not nihilistic.

But now, Jay said he didn't know what he wanted to do, so the plan was no plan. That's also a lot like the Fool card.

"I am doing the bare minimum until I figure it out . . ." he said, oblivious, or maybe not caring, that he was on track to never figure it out.

The Hanged Man's card is number twelve. It is the opposite of the card for success and completion, number twenty-one, the World. As the Hanged Man hangs, his world is indeed upside down.

"The thing is, Julia, I don't know how to do anything well enough," he said. "I don't know how to live."

I would not let myself feel sorry for him because no sooner did I sympathize than his mood would swing to the other extreme.

He pointed at other lives, lives that he viewed as mediocre. Jay considered the masses with contempt and disgust. He would never lower himself to *that,* to have to wear nice clothes ("a costume") to go to work, get a degree, or do whatever must be done. Society would not dictate who Jay needed to be. He felt superior in the truth of who he was. But who was Jay? What was he doing? He couldn't decide.

Eventually, Jay did get his GED. He even signed up at the community college and took an English class. Jay was better read than almost any adult I knew. Pick a classic, and he had probably read it. Jay usually had a great novel, some philosophical treatise, and maybe a book on the occult or some offbeat subject in his backpack. He was brilliant; only it was brilliance with no personal discipline or practical application. Jay could have written the required essays in fifteen minutes in his English class. But he let himself fail because he didn't—wouldn't—get around to finishing them.

"They weren't *true,*" he told me. "I tell the truth. I tell the truth because there's no one to impress. I needed words that were worthy of putting on paper. Otherwise, what's the point?"

I tell the truth because there's no one to impress. I couldn't decide if that was genius or utter bullshit. I wondered if I should feel insulted.

"The point is," I said, "you need to prove to your school that you can do it. The point is that you go through the required bullshit to move on to what *will* inspire you. The point is not to choose to be a failure. Why are you *choosing* that?" My voice rose in exasperation. I sounded like every other closed-minded adult.

Some say the mythology behind the Hanged Man references the Norse god Odin, who hung upside down for nine days and nights, sacrificing himself *for* himself. Some say the Hanged Man is Judas Iscariot, the betrayer of Jesus. And some see the Hanged Man, who hangs from his gallows on a Tau Cross, as Jesus. Every story is about sacrificing the self for something higher. The problem with Jay was that he didn't have a higher purpose.

Jay's eyes looked watery and close to crying.

"I'm not choosing to be a failure, Julia! I'm choosing *not to choose* until I'm sure. I don't want to do something I'm going to regret forever. I don't want to create something that will embarrass me. I don't choose failure. Failure is just a by-product. I don't even know who I *am* yet. How can I choose anything? I'm barely a character in my own life. Maybe I'm just scenery."

The Hanged Man is the opposite energy to the Hierophant card. As the Hierophant seeks fame and society's external connections and acclaim, the Hanged Man looks inward. He sacrifices for the divinity of mystical experience. The Hanged Man requires a change of consciousness, or he must suffer the consequences of never attaining a satisfying life. The next card in the Major Arcana's sequence is Death. Change has to happen.

"Then *be* scenery, Jay. Just be something! You're almost thirty. You're disappearing. You're turning into nothing. When will you paint again? When will you play the guitar?"

"When I can learn to breathe," he said.

And with that, I took a breath for him, gathered my cards, kissed him on the cheek, and left him to figure it out on his own.

The Basics

Learn the fundamental meanings of the symbols, and the rest comes easily. The numbers all have associations: Aces are beginnings; Twos are partnerships; Fives are conflict, and so on. If you learn the meaning of the Major Arcana cards, they can inform you about the meanings of numbers of the Minors. For instance, the Four of a focused Emperor reflects that Emperor's traits of order and balance, without emotion, across the Minor Arcana suits in the rank of the Fours. You will find this information online or in any good tarot book.

It's also essential to learn the traits of the suits: Cups are love and emotion; Wands are creativity; Swords are reason, logic, and action; Pentacles are materials and things of the world.

Everything hinges upon these basics.

13
DEATH

I pulled up to the midtown nursing home, an unimpressive, dingy brick structure adjoining an old church. Someone had made a weak attempt at landscaping, and a few stray daisies clung to life as the midautumn cold approached. All one level, with small windows that angled out partially for ventilation, I would have guessed this building to be an elementary school if not for the signage. Perhaps it once was.

It was a Halloween party, known as *Samhain* to my Wiccan friends who keep the Celtic and Gaelic traditions alive. Samhain marks the time between the times: the halfway point between autumnal equinox and winter solstice denotes the harvest season's end and introduces the darker half of a year measured by thirteen moons. And so the Death card, number thirteen in the Major Arcana, with its gray sky and bare ground, represents this dark half-season of winter.

When I'm hired as the entertainment for parties in nursing homes and assisted living centers, I know that I will do some heavy spiritual work, no matter how superficially bright and happy the administration tries to make the event. The fact is that people in nursing homes don't have a lot to look forward to, and so there is quite a bit of depression, hopelessness, and loneliness. The more expensive homes in the suburbs are shiny and new, with a constant parade of musicians and entertainers like me brought in around their resident bingo games and chair massages. The less opulent homes are in older buildings like this one, with cream-painted cinder block walls and gray-green fluorescent lighting that reminded me of feeling trapped in a high school classroom. Ah, but these were not high schools, and the only youth present were the staff, who talked to the patients in the same sing-song, patronizing voices used to talk to a puppy or a child. The one thing all of the patients have in common is that they have lost a great deal, if not all, of their dignity as their bodies and minds begin to fade and fail.

The Death card is read as a card of transformation and rebirth. Death is a card that says that the old life is behind you, and you are in a whole new place. The Death card seldom symbolizes literal death, although it can on occasion. And this event would likely be one of those occasions.

The staff had me situated in the center of the cafeteria, at one of twenty or more 1960s-style round Formica tables, the kind with sparkles poured into the surface. There was a spread at the back of the room with Halloween cookies and heated stainless steel pots with the day's planned lunch, some kind of soup or stew. "Monster Mash" played loudly over the PA, and some residents jiggled and shuffled around, attempting to dance in costume in the adjoining room.

Halloween and Samhain are regarded as an especially magical twenty-four hours. During this same window of time, Mexico celebrates the Day of the Dead, when friends and relatives who have passed on rise again to walk among the living. Like the Death card, the season is a time of transition. Winter was considered the "season of ghosts" in these religions, and the autumnal celebrations were their spirits' release from the Underworld. Halloween costumes were originally a strategic plan to confuse ghosts, demons, fairies, and witches. They wouldn't hurt you if you were one of them, right?

The cafeteria workers, all Bosnian refugees, raced to my table to have their cards read before the staff noticed or the residents had a sense of my purpose there and became interested themselves. All dressed in white uniforms and with their hair pulled up and back in hairnets, each kitchen worker told me their name in broken English: "I am Zara," "I am Džejla," "I am Adna." These women were old-school Muslims and devoted to their families. Each one selflessly asked the same questions: if their men and sons would be successful and if their daughters would marry well.

The Death card can be marriage, babies being born, or other joyful occasions when everything is suddenly different. Unfortunately, however, I had little good news to share with these immigrant workers, as each of their lives had been swallowed up by cards of war and death. Over and over, I saw the Emperor reversed, the Ten of Swords, the Four of Swords reversed, the Tower, and of course, the Death card. The Death card was the only tarot card they recognized, or maybe they just made their assumptions about it, which anyone might do. We have all seen it: that grinning skeleton wearing a suit of black armor, riding a white horse. In some renderings, he holds the Grim Reaper's scythe. In the traditional deck, the one I used that day, he holds a flag of the Rosicrucians, who practice alchemy. In the picture on the card, the horse tramples the dead and dying bodies, who are young, old, and even of religious and social importance. A crown lies in the mud. A pope begs for mercy. Children weep. No one is spared from Death; he is always victorious.

I saw fear on their faces, and I tried to explain through the language barrier.

"No, this is not now. This was your home. Where you come from. *Bosnia.*" I pointed to the Death card. I then put my hands on my heart. "You need to heal. Too much hurt. Do you understand?"

They nodded, more out of polite obligation than understanding.

"Money?" one of them asked.

There were no money cards. No hint of a pentacle anywhere.

"I'm sorry, not today," I said. And then trying again, "Is there someone you can talk to? A counselor? A doctor? An Imam? About the war?"

They looked at me blankly with each reading, trying to process my words.

It's important to remember that the Death card is number thirteen of twenty-two. Death is not the end. Death is just a step in our growth. It is the death of old beliefs, emotions, and ways of life to create something new and better. Through the Death card, we grow wiser.

The administrators shooed the workers back to the kitchen. This was a party for the residents.

I was initially shocked to learn that not all nursing home residents are old. First to be seated at my circular table with its glittery sparkles was a man named Fred, around my age. Reasonably nice looking, I would have assumed he was there visiting a resident or another worker if it were not for the drool that ran out of the corner of his mouth. He had had the misfortune of a stroke.

"Just tell me when I will get out of here," Fred said.

This would be an occasion that we would *want* to see the Death card, which can also mean change; when the old life is behind us and everything is new. If you look carefully at the Death card picture, the sun rises in the distance between two towers, which represent New Jerusalem. The Death card is often read as a card of those milestones in life when everything changes for the better: graduation, marriage, children born, retirement. On the negative side, it can mean the end of a career, divorce, and of course, death.

For Fred, I saw the Hanged Man. He wasn't going anywhere anytime soon.

A resident named Linda sat down next. She was a plump woman with long dishwater-brown hair with bangs like a little girl. She was dressed like a witch with a floppy brimmed, black pointed hat and a black polyester dress. Her overall demeanor and her nervous giggle made her appear much younger than her sixty years, if she had told me the truth about her age.

Linda leaned over toward me and whispered, "I'm not supposed to be here."

"You're not?" I said. "What happened?"

"They made a mistake. I said the wrong thing, and they made a mistake."

"What did you say?" I asked. She seemed to want to tell me.

"Well, my grandchildren were getting on my nerves, you know?

And I told my doctor that I really, really, really wanted to kill them."

Her energy amped up with every "really," and her voice became more aggressive. I sat stunned for a moment.

"Yes, that was probably the wrong thing to say."

"Tell me my fortune?" she asked, immediately brightening at the prospect of a happy future.

I shuffled the cards hesitantly.

"Linda, this is the Hermit card. He goes off on his own and considers his life and where it is going. I think that you are here in this place to think about how words can hurt and scare people. Does that make sense?"

"That's a lot of hooey!" she said, standing up abruptly and leaving the table to return to the dance floor.

Just as Jesus dies and, after three days, is resurrected in Christianity, most religions and mystical traditions have stories, rituals, or meanings around death. In alchemy, death, represented by the white rose of the Rosicrucian flag on the Death card, is the necessary destruction of the base material to become pure. Among the ancient Egyptians, the Greek Eleusinians, Mexicans, and Hindus and in shamanistic rituals across the world, there are ceremonies to face Death and willingly surrender to nature's forces.

Giovanni was the next resident to sit before me. He was an extremely well-dressed, handsome elderly Black man. Giovanni wore a vest over a pressed long-sleeve button-down shirt, with cufflinks and even a tiny handkerchief artfully folded into his breast pocket. He wore equally stylish pressed trousers and shined-up loafers. This man took time on the little details, which told me he was still connected to the outside world. Or at least, he wanted to be.

"What would you like to know?" I asked him as I shuffled the cards.

"What is there to know?" he said. "I can't even go for a walk outside. I might fall or something. I hardly ever get visitors. I can't stand television. We are all just sitting here, waiting to die."

I listened, holding the cards but not placing any of them down on the table. No cards were going to change that awful fact.

"For a man as pulled together as you are, you must be living for something, eh? Do you have friends here?"

"Some. But you know, it's like the war. You don't want to get too attached because people are dropping every day."

Giovanni was too sincere to play polite games with. I gave it to him straight.

"Giovanni, you know when Shakespeare said, 'All the world's a stage, and we are merely players'? Well, that is a tenet of mysticism. I believe that we are all connected, all one, and standing together on the other side. Over here, in the world, this is our stage. I get to put on the mask and be Julia the Tarot Card Reader, and you get to be Giovanni, the Resident. Because you're older than me, unless I have a tragedy, your time on stage will end before mine because you started before me. But here's the thing: this is the playground. This is where we learn and become our best selves. Our bodies are going to crap out on us, and we are going to die because they are not built for forever. But science has proven that energy doesn't die. It just goes somewhere else. That's the substantial you. Your essence. Your soul. Whether you want to embrace Heaven or reincarnation or just being in a peaceful place is totally your business. I will never tell you what to believe. I just want to say right now that I think you're very cool and definitely on the ball, and I am very sorry to see you have to go through this misery because you, my friend, deserve better. But maybe you can find some good in it? Maybe there is some kind of positive you can create?"

Giovanni gave a weak smile and set his hand down in front of me. I reached over and held his hand for a long minute. I never put a single card down for him. I didn't need to.

A deejay had taken over and begun playing music in the adjoining room. He blasted Cher's "If I Could Turn Back Time" and the crowd hollered the words out like a drunken mass on New Year's Eve. Next up was the Eagles' "Hotel California," with that unforgettable line, "You can check out any time you like, but you can never leave."

Oh, Giovanni! "Hotel California" felt like his song. And Fred's. And even Linda's. It hurt to know how true it was. It gave me gratitude for my health and youth, which is moving past fast, but I am still well in middle age, if not young. My Death cards of the future will hopefully be grandchildren and retirement. May my vigor remain a long time, and bless my petty complaints. We always take it for granted until we lose it.

My two hours were up, and I gathered my tarot cards back into their boxes and stored them in my little treasure chest. The staff banged their pots and pans as they cleared the buffet table and sprayed everything down with disinfectant. The residents continued dancing and shuffling about, now to "Devil Woman" by Cliff Richard. It all felt incomplete, but at least, unlike the residents, I got to leave. Does Death ever feel right?

And Giovanni? I look forward to seeing him again on the other side.

Sympathetic Resonance

I have learned that when I am reminded of something from my own life, if I *feel* a story in the cards relates to something that has happened to me or to someone I know, I have to share this with my clients. It has risen to my consciousness to be told. The circumstances may be different, but the emotions are all there, and my feelings are their feelings. I express what happened for both of us, and the person I'm reading for applies their own interpretation. A medium I know calls this Sympathetic Resonance. The tarot card reader and client read these cards together, and I think it is proof that we are all one.

14
TEMPERANCE

I didn't listen to my intuition, which said to stay home and relax. Maybe get some reading and writing done, and start packing for my upcoming trip to the beach. But my phone rang, and a little girlish voice on the other end asked if I had any in-person session time open for a tarot card reading that evening. As much as I would have preferred to take it easy, I thought it would be a good idea to get a little more work done before I left town. I committed to meet this girl named Kelsey and her male friend at a nearby coffee shop at 7:15 p.m.

The Temperance card features an effulgent, red-winged angel holding two chalices, pouring water into wine. Some say this card depicts the goddess Iris, the messenger of the gods and goddess of the rainbow. She pours wine, but my favorite gods and goddesses pour coffee and tea. These, too, are magic elixirs.

I always grab a table against the wall or in the corner to get a bit of privacy. I've learned. In the past, I'd set cards out on tables amid everything, and random people thought I was performing some kind of a show. They didn't hesitate to walk up and interrupt with questions. And so that evening, I selected a table against the window, waiting with my herbal tea while I surfed my phone for a bit. Our appointment for 7:15 came and went. I caught up on my email and read an article about organizing closets. My rule was to wait no longer than fifteen minutes. Right at 7:30 p.m., as I started to get up and write this one off as a no-show, my cellphone rang. It was Kelsey.

"I'm sorry! We got lost! The GPS says we'll be there in thirteen minutes. Can you wait?"

Well, I was already there and I was just lounging and comfortable, so I said yes.

Some schools of thought combine the Temperance card with the idea of Prudence. Temperance/Prudence is considered one of the virtues: being cautious and careful. Other tarot scholars look at the Hermit as representing Prudence and Temperance as its own thing, mostly self-control. Temperance is considered to be the messenger between Spirit and the Earth. She processes what is perceived and determines what we do with that information. We ultimately choose how we think and react. And when we do personal growth work, we begin to choose how we process our thoughts. As my waiting time increased, my processes and perceptions became less and less favorable for Kelsey.

Another fifteen minutes passed. I texted Kelsey, telling her that I would leave if she did not show up by 8:00 p.m. It was getting ridiculous. Altogether, I had already waited for forty-five unpaid minutes. When people don't respect my time, I become resentful. I could have been helping someone else or packing for the beach. I had an abundance of items on my to-do list and did not have time to be sitting around waiting on some kid.

At 8:00 p.m., I packed up, walked to my car, and drove home, listening to my favorite Buddhist master, Pema Chodron, on audiobook. *Breathe in anger and frustration,* Chodron encouraged. *Breathe out peace and tranquility.* I practiced. *Breathe in,* knowing that other people in the world felt just as infuriated for people wasting their precious time. *Breathe out* gratitude that I was not alone and doing peace work to heal others who also felt this. *Breathe in* that I felt anger and hatred. *Breathe out* that it was just an annoyance and would all be forgotten when I got to the beach. I did the breathing. I reached my home and pulled my car into the garage.

Before I could turn off my car, my phone rang again. It was Kelsey. I didn't want to answer it, but I did. Answering my phone is like a religious obligation or something. I need to let go of the guilt of ignoring people.

"Hello."

"We're here! I'm so sorry!" she trilled. One can only hear *so sorry* a certain number of times before it doesn't mean anything anymore.

The flowing water on the Temperance card's picture represents the flow of time. *My time,* in this case. Temperance's Roman numeral XIV, or fourteen, is associated with energy, sexuality, and continuous change. It is the alchemical balance of male and female sexual forces. Temperance follows the Death card in the Major Arcana, and the new life created by Death must have moderation, balance, and flow.

"I couldn't wait any longer," I said. I was not in the mood. I had to pack, and I was tired. I would love and serve humanity tomorrow. Maybe. That night, I had decided that I didn't like her and didn't care what happened.

"Can you come *back?*" she asked in her pleading, high-pitched little girl voice.

"No. Sorry. I waited for forty-five minutes, and it's late now. If you want to schedule something again, you'll need to pay me for the time you missed. *And* my travel time. I could have been working for someone else."

"I'm so sorry," she muttered.

"Good night," I said, and I hung up.

Stupid kids. Breathe. Breathe. Breathe. I thought of a million errands I could have completed in that forty-five minutes, which now felt more precious than ever. Gone! Temperance, the card under the sign of Sagittarius, is a higher state of awareness. It is becoming conscious of Spirit in physical life. Me? I was all too conscious of my physical life, this inconvenience upon me, and most especially of my dead temporal time.

In less than a minute, my phone rang again. Kelsey's number. Ugh. I considered letting it ring, but then I picked it up, from habit, I guess. I didn't even give my professional greeting. Temperance can be a card to restore harmony or mediate a situation, but I didn't care anymore.

"Yeah?"

Now there was a man's voice on the line. He sounded older. Maybe her father?

"Hey, what if we pay you for the time you waited? Will you meet us then?"

"Well, Starbucks is going to close. . . ."

"Meet us somewhere else?"

"Did you come from a long way?" I asked. I began to soften, and it sounded like they would make it up to me.

"Yeah."

I said I would.

My husband, Tom, stood in the kitchen, putting dirty dishes into the dishwasher while eavesdropping on my interrupted entry and a quick exit from the house.

"I don't have a good feeling about this," he said.

I never even had the chance to put my purse and jacket down. I told them to meet me at the McDonald's across the parking lot from where we had originally agreed to meet and pivoted back toward my car in the garage. That McDonald's is bright and safe, albeit empty at night, and it's new and a little more upscale than their regular locations.

It took me ten minutes to drive back, and it should have taken them no time to run or even walk across the parking lot. It was a ghost town when I walked in, save for the lone young girl behind the counter, talking to a car at the drive-through window through a headset. My clients were nowhere to be seen. I hung out in the corner like I was casing the joint. What the hell?

I called Kelsey's phone number. This unsaved sequence of digits had so many recent calls on my phone. The man answered again.

"Yeah?"

"Um, I'm here in McDonald's," I said, voice trailing off, implying, "and where the hell are you?"

"She'll be right in," he said and hung up.

I waited for five interminable minutes. The blackness of the empty nighttime parking lot around this neon-bright yellow island of

McDonald's felt somehow sickening. There was no sign of her. I texted my husband: *I think they're fucking with me.* Just what kind of person got their kicks arranging false meetings? Teenagers, that's who. I wanted to kill them. When would I learn to read my own tarot cards and screen these losers?

Suddenly, a very made-up blonde woman stumbled in the door. *This* was Kelsey. She was not a teenager. Kelsey was one of those women who might be in her twenties or her forties. Like Temperance, she was a blend of every age. Hard to tell. She had definitely been drinking. *Temperance* is a word they used during the Prohibition, stressing balance and moderation.

"Hi!" she giggled, tottering in her high heels and size 2 designer jeans. Judging from the getup and the generous view of her softball-sized breasts, I guessed she might be a stripper. She looked the part.

The man trailed after her. He was short, maybe sixty years old, with a baseball cap, a three-day beard, and blue-collar work clothes. He reached into his pocket and gave me a one-hundred-dollar bill and twenty bucks cash from a brass money clip.

"Just a half-hour," he ordered to the both of us. The one-twenty didn't exactly cover all of my time lost *plus* half an hour, but it was close enough.

Kelsey slumped sideways in the bright-yellow plastic molded restaurant booth seat, and at the same time, she appeared jittery and twitchy. Her eyes were heavily lined with black liner, her eyelids shaded in dark metallic red copper. Kelsey's hair was the dry blonde of straw bales, and her lips were a shiny, dark red. This chick was a disaster.

"Choose your deck," I instructed, motioning at the wooden chest I had set on the table, which held my assortment of tarot card boxes. I hoped that the half hour would go by quickly. Meanwhile, Kelsey said at full volume so that her gentleman friend would hear, "Oh, I wish I had more time!" He ignored her.

I play a game with myself at every reading, guessing which deck my client will pick. I am almost always correct. It took her several minutes of looking them over, but Kelsey chose the *Cosmic Tarot,* as I thought she would. It was the most psychedelic-looking deck of the bunch. Felt right.

The angel on the Temperance card mixes the waters of life. These waters are considered sexual, medicinal, alchemical, and philosophical. Each property of water has a light side and a dark side. As the Temperance card is in the second tarot cycle of tens, she demonstrates how to achieve all aspects of a perfect union for the Lovers. I was having trouble uniting my energies to Kelsey, however. I wasn't entirely conscious of it, but I had decided that we were too different, and I would not like her.

I instructed Kelsey to shuffle the cards. Her long red fingernails fluttered the deck into a sloppy bridge, impeded by the chunky gold and diamond rings she wore on almost every finger. But I couldn't criticize anyone's shuffling. I have been reading the cards for over forty years, and I still can't shuffle. Tarot cards are bigger than regular cards, and there are seventy-eight of them. Kelsey wasted a lot of her half-hour's time, which was fine by me. She was not there for spiritual growth or enlightenment. She was there to see if her wishes would come true.

"Can you go somewhere else, pleeeeease?" Kelsey said to her male friend in her cutest put-on voice. "I need priiiiiiivacy!"

He looked momentarily irritated and then humored her and stepped outside. When he was gone, I gave her the spiel about how I start with a general reading. This reveals a little bit of the past, present, and future. From there, she can see what's up, and we can answer questions. The card at her core was the Eight of Swords, the woman in the cage. I told her she feels trapped, enslaved to the Devil in reverse, which was her crossing card.

"But look," I said. "That woman can't see, because she's blindfolded, that the door is open. She can walk out at any time. She just doesn't know that she has other options."

Kelsey nodded woozily. Enlightenment is not for the weak of heart. Or for the drunk of mind.

I saw a King of Pentacles in reverse, standing around in her near future. He was going to dump her.

"Your meal ticket is running out," I said, and I cast my eyes over toward the door where that man stood looking at his phone. She shrugged. She knew it wasn't forever.

Some read the Temperance card as a card of motion, and in reverse, it is a motion toward destruction. I think of Sylvia Plath's poem "Ariel," which corresponds to this tarot card. But in addition to Plath's poem speaking about a horseback riding session in Dartmoor, it also summed up the bombings of Hiroshima and Nagasaki.*

The rest of Kelsey's tarot reading was pretty much what I expected, although there was a problem overshadowing her life—the subject of children. Either she had difficult children or wanted children, which was difficult for her. I did not want to imagine this woman as a mother.

"Tell me about my boyfriend, Freddy," she said, her hand excitedly slamming down on the cards. She was alarmed at the volume of her own voice and looked around to see if the guy she was with might have heard but he was still outside. What I knew for sure was that guy was *not* Freddy.

The Four of Swords reversed told me things weren't happy. I said it's a card of severe depression and isolation, sometimes of being locked up in hospitals or prisons. "Things you can't get out of," I explained.

"Yeah, he's in jail," she said in a casual tone that she might have instead said he was lying on the couch watching TV.

"Freddy will be out within a year, but he is not with you forever."

"It figures," she said, too loud again. "Tell me what you see with him and someone named Joanne." She hissed out the other woman's name.

I put the cards down.

"Hmmm. I'm just going to call it as I see it, but I am not sure *what* I see exactly. I'll talk us both through it: Freddy shows up as a Knight of Wands in reverse. He can't be trusted and is not faithful. But there is this Queen of Cups in reverse. Sometimes these queens are mothers, but she doesn't show up as a mother in these cards. She does feel older. . . ."

---

*Julia Gordon-Bramer, *Fixed Stars Govern a Life: Decoding Sylvia Plath* (Nacogdoches, Tex.: Stephen F. Austin State University Press, 2014), 131–40.

Kelsey wanted to get to the point. "Did Freddy sleep with Joanne?"

I put down more cards. They were piled up on the table, rows upon rows, a mess of color and symbol. I had a "No" for Kelsey's question, yet there was some doubt. The Lovers reversed, *and* the Page of Wands reversed told me there was some impropriety between Freddy and Joanne. The High Priestess said that this was something that they would rather keep quiet. And since the cards had been pushed around, now the Queen of Cups' head was on the Knight of Wands' staff. I started to laugh.

"Um . . ."

"Say it!" she demanded. Her voice had grown up. It was deeper and huskier. Kelsey was at least forty.

I pointed at what I saw.

"I think Joanne gave Freddy a blow job."

We both started to laugh at the fact I said it so crudely. I continued, "So, well, no, it wasn't sex, *per se*. Not in the fullest sense of the word. It was sex in the Bill Clinton sense." (I knew by now that she was old enough to remember the nineties.)

Ah, Temperance! The card of mixing opposites. I had found how to connect with this woman, after all. We could both enjoy a dirty joke, and neither of us was too shy to get to the point.

Kelsey told me that made sense. This Joanne was a friend of Freddy's mother, and Joanne had taken Freddy in to live with her, gave him money, and treated him like a prince. It was all there, in the Six of Pentacles, with its rich man giving to beggars, and the Seven of Swords, which is the thief running off with the loot. When Freddy was not in jail, he took what he could get. He was riding the gravy train. I didn't see that changing anytime soon.

Our half an hour was almost up.

"Let me just ask you one more thing," Kelsey said, her voice turning young and sweet again. "Am I ever going to have children?"

Oh yes, I remembered how the Page of Cups in reverse had started this whole reading. It wasn't that Kelsey was worried over children. It was that she wanted to have them. But she was rather alone in the world. And in my judgment, she was not equipped to care for anyone, including herself. I added cards.

Kelsey saw for herself that the spread did not look encouraging: The Nine of Swords is a woman crying alone in a dark room. There was that terrifying Tower card, with its lightning bolt and bodies falling off the building. The unknown limbo of the Hanged Man and the exile of the Hermit. No, it did not look good.

"Kelsey, you have a lot of dark energy around you," I said, trying to be gentle.

"I know!" she almost hollered back, putting her hand on mine. So this wasn't just another *will-I-win-the-lottery?* type of reading. Maybe something I said that night would help her. I could hope.

"You won't have children unless a lot of things change in your life. You are with scary people right now. You have addiction issues, and this Temperance card reversed? That's about your health. But it's upside down. You are not living the kind of life to have children. Nothing is in your favor for it: not your health, not your relationships, not your finances. Temperance means balance and moderation. Girl, I don't see you doing *anything* in balance and moderation, and I see you suffer for it. I am sorry. But everything and anything *can* be changed. It's possible. You just have to want it enough."

Kelsey gave a sad shrug, which told me she wanted kids, but not *that* much. I remembered some parties in the past where I read tarot for people who were drunk or using other substances. It never went well. At their best, the inebriated holler everything at me, slur their speech, and repeat themselves. At their worst, they begin to read the cards themselves in horror or misunderstand what I say and burst into tears. I've had some clients get hysterical. Occasionally someone will get aggressive and challenge me on it. And people think my work is a piece of cake!

The red wings of the angel on the Temperance card are about elevating our issues to a higher nature. This is what happens when we reconcile our opposites. I had been elevated by meeting Kelsey, even though initially I didn't want that experience. Kelsey got to imagine some options for herself, and we both shared a laugh.

Given all this, Kelsey was remarkably self-possessed. She had her problems, sure. But Kelsey owned them and was kind of OK even though some of her dreams weren't coming true. She had her sugar daddy for now. Freddy would be out of jail soon. And kids? Well, they might cramp her style. After all, life is short. Hers especially.

Changing Your Future

One of the most important things you must know about the tarot is that nothing is set in stone, and your future can be corrected if you don't like what a reading says. You are never doomed, because you have the power to do some things differently.

What's the point of the tarot, then? you might ask. The purpose of the tarot is to show you the track you're on. Nothing more. That's why I hate the "fortune teller" label. It's more like a compass pointing you in the right direction than a treasure map showing you that X marks the spot.

We all know so much more about ourselves than we consciously realize. We know when we're leading ourselves into trouble, falling into old habits and addictions, and deluding ourselves or others out of insecurities and need. Likewise, we know when we've fallen into our groove and doing what we are called to do. The cards reflect it to you. It's a mirror. If you don't like the reflection for tomorrow, change what you're doing today.

15

THE DEVIL

Ana Sofia and Alejandra were two ravishing Latinas who emigrated from Colombia to St. Louis ten years ago. All fashion and opulence, they kept themselves looking an indeterminate age, eternally young. Over my years reading their tarot cards, I estimated that they were both around forty years old, but each easily looked thirty.

Allow me to present the tarot card of the Devil. The Devil represents the material world and sensual pleasures. People see me turn over the Devil in their tarot spread and they panic. *Relax,* I tell them. *This isn't about being evil; it's about being indulgent.* We all love the Devil. When he's right side up, that is. The Devil is about "living large": good food, drink, pretty clothes, expensive cars, sex, vacations, sleeping late . . . you get the picture.

Ana Sofia was the quiet one, with sunny golden blonde hair, milk chocolate eyes, and Brigitte Bardot lips. She had less to say because she had more to lose. Alejandra was a striking, tall, glamorous woman with waist-length caramel hair and the kind of body seen on pinup girls in the 1950s and '60s. Both reminded me of Hollywood vixens with their darkened, shaped eyebrows, thick black eyelash extensions, and perfect red lips. They were each other's best friends and partners in crime as they traveled the world together, jetting off to Dubai or Cancun or Paris, always flying first class, letting wealthy men pay for and entertain them, and living the life. Their Instagram accounts made them the envy of everyone as they pouted and blew kisses in front of every tourist attraction.

Ana Sofia and Alejandra shared that Latina fashion of speaking that is both rapid and languorous, with long stretches of syllables, rolling *R's,* and more words crammed into thirty seconds than an English-speaking North American could possibly manage.

"Hooo-lia! Girrrl, I need my tarrrot cards! Bring your sooooot-case, please. I have meeny questions," Ana Sofia said on my voicemail when she wanted me to come to her office and give them a reading. But don't let the sorority house colloquialisms fool you. These women were no dummies. Ana Sofia and Alejandra worked long hours at multiple jobs: fashion merchandising, hairdressing, selling jewelry, all while they attended school, advancing their degrees. And, of course, they were professional gold diggers. Totally right for the Devil, who is about the material world but not all that interested in the spiritual.

When I read tarot cards, I sometimes see things that I initially don't understand. For instance, the first time I read in the office for Ana Sofia, I saw her as definitely married, but it looked like she was married to two people. This made no sense because bigamy was not legal, here or in Colombia, as far as I knew. I explained my confusion to her.

"An affair, I presume? No judgment. I'm only trying to get clear here," I said. I have lived long enough to know that every relationship is complicated, and every marriage has its ups and downs.

"David is my husband, but . . ." Ana Sofia stopped short. She never revealed too much. She always wanted to see what I could see already. David was the Knight of Pentacles in reverse, a guy who had no direction or ambition. And there was Ana Sofia, represented by the Devil card, with her expensive tastes. I did not tell her she was the Devil, or even, on some days, the impossible to please Queen of Pentacles reversed. I doubt it would have bothered her much if I had.

The Devil card pictures a naked couple chained to the great bat-winged, goat-headed beast Baphomet. The man and woman both have horns and tails. The woman's tail ends with a bunch of grapes at its tip and the man's ends in flames. This is a moralistic lesson about the addictive qualities of the Devil and of sexual relationships, which may turn sour or burn us in the end. There is always a price to pay when we let the Devil run the show.

"So this other man," I said, "who is not David, he is a King of Pentacles. Wealthy. And you show as married to him too."

She held up a hunky diamond ring on a perfectly manicured hand. "Fifty," she said with a naughty smile.

"Thousand?" I asked. She nodded.

"And David doesn't ask about this ring?"

"He think eets fake."

On another occasion, Ana Sofia pulled back her cornsilk hair to show off her new diamond earrings.

"Thirrrty thousand," she purred.

And so, over these years, it came out that the "boyfriend," Marcus, was a wealthy older lawyer. He paid Ana Sofia's tuition costs, which were not cheap, and kept her living in high style. She drove a Caldera Red Jaguar and had a side business outside of her work at the salon. Marcus paid for all of it.

The Devil card can represent someone who wants to buy love and affection. It's a sad situation for both parties because it's a game of control, not the love the buyer is after. And the person bought by the Devil has sold their soul for the material world. Thus the chains on the couple show that they are in a prison of their own making.

Sometimes the Devil card describes an intense, addictive relationship that we sense is dangerous yet is impossible to let go of. We can feel bound to the person and unable to leave, no matter how poorly we are treated.

Thirty thousand dollars for a pair of earrings! Whew. That was more than the cost of my car. Long ago, I realized I probably looked pretty shabby compared to those two. For a while, I used to dress up when I saw them. Eventually I quit trying. Now all I did was comb my hair and check that there wasn't food in my teeth.

Marcus bought a house for himself and Ana Sofia, and Ana Sofia lived half the time with him there. When Ana Sofia was not in school or work or traveling with Alejandra, she traveled with Marcus. She told David that she was "going to conferences." The cards showed David knew something was up. He had to know. But he wanted to keep her, and the lifestyle worked pretty well for him too, as he preferred to stay at home with his electronics.

Like the Lovers card, the Devil can represent intensity and obsession. The trouble with the Devil in this territory is that things get weird and ugly. The Devil misuses his power and controls others to get what he wants, and he often gets greedy, selfish, and even possessed as he pursues money, power, and status.

When it was Alejandra's turn with the tarot cards, she mainly asked about Stanley and if he was presently cheating on her. Stanley was also fabulously wealthy, a foot shorter and twenty years older than Alejandra, and it had come out in his cards that he was a sex addict (the Devil in reverse and the Moon in reverse). Alejandra was willing to endure it all if she could marry him without a prenup.

"Eh, tell me something I don't know," Alejandra said. "He es going to destroy himself." Stanley is a banker, and he is friends with Marcus. Alejandra knew that Stanley had been having an affair with his twenty-five-year-old married receptionist for the last several months, as well as whoever else was interested.

"She es too skinny and has no taste!" Alejandra hissed about the receptionist. Before this girl, Alejandra discovered that Stanley had been having flings with a female doctor. "She es not even pretty!" Alejandra said with disgust. She showed me their pictures on Facebook and then scanned through the photos on her phone to show me a picture she took walking behind the receptionist and Stanley when the three of them were at the airport. Alejandra had invited herself along to a conference to monitor his behavior.

"Look at herrr! Look at those trashy jeans! It was five degrees that day! And herrr eye makeup!"

I looked at the picture on Alejandra's phone. The girl's jeans were laced down the side, leaving a lot of skin showing from thigh to ankle.

Her head was turned to the side, but she wore heavy dark eye shadow and eyeliner that made her look decades older than she was. I had to admit, yes, the jeans were trashy. And yes, the girl's makeup was awful. If Alejandra's got one thing going for her, she's got style.

Alejandra scrolled to another photo. "And now look at me, so pretty!" she smiled proudly. And yeah, she was, in her diamonds and furs and perfect makeup. Rita Hayworth, eat your heart out.

Alejandra and Stanley were officially engaged and had been living together for several years. Alejandra converted to Judaism for him, and I think she enjoyed going to temple because it was all high society there, and she could dress to impress. Alejandra and Stanley went back and forth about that prenuptial agreement. Stanley always presented it to her as a pragmatic and beneficial thing, but when she read the fine print, he wanted her to sign something that said she wouldn't get anything at all if they didn't work out. That was not agreeable to Alejandra. She had a daughter from another marriage, she was a cancer survivor, and she had expensive tastes. Her salary alone would not be enough to cover her clothes and her shining black Porsche with its license plate that read: "B CHIC."

The Devil card is a counterpart to the Hierophant, seen in the first ten cards of the tarot's Major Arcana. The Hierophant is the spiritual ruler, and the Devil rules the material world. The trick is to live in both worlds but not be consumed by either.

Half the time, Alejandra and Stanley couldn't stand each other, but the other half they did seem to work. Stanley called them a "power couple," and that they were, appearing in the spotlight at all the swanky events, getting their pictures in society pages while showing their sunniest smiles to the world, no matter what they'd been through privately. Alejandra said that if she were ever to leave Stanley, it wouldn't happen until after she finished school because he had to pay for it. That was the plan. A rich man in Dubai also wanted to marry her, and she visited him on occasion when he bought her a ticket, but he was already married. She would not be a second wife to anyone. She was always looking. Stanley's tarot cards showed that regardless of his relationship with

Alejandra, he liked her as a trophy. She was his reward for being successful. He enjoyed knowing that body was in his bed and that all men wished they were him.

Over those years of reading their cards, I grew fond of Ana Sofia and Alejandra. I can't say I understand why. Maybe it is the amusement factor. Their stories were better than any TV show, and I often told them this. We were all friends on Facebook. Ana Sofia's profile was set up so that she looked very single, with not a hint of a man in her life. She posted only pictures of her travels with Alejandra or various fancy parties or events she attended. Alejandra's profile featured nothing but photos of her and Stanley. One *would* think that they were the dream couple. I knew the truth. And I do not know what life was like growing up in Colombia. This is a subject neither woman spoke of, but when I looked at the cards, I saw the Five of Pentacles, which is poverty. Poverty is anathema to Ana Sofia and Alejandra today. It is a thing so evil, so horrible, that they were willing to do anything to flee as far from it as possible. The tragedy is that they seek happiness in the Devil, and the Devil says, *Seek and keep seeking; you'll never find it*. The Devil is a drug, and there can never be enough.

When the Devil card shows up in reverse, I consider it one of the worst cards in the deck. Addiction, depression, panic, and anxiety . . . these are the traits of the Devil in reverse. Everything wrong with our world today stems from the qualities of this card. Qabalah suggests that these symptoms all stem from one thing: *pain*. Pain that we don't want to feel, and so we stuff it down and keep stuffing it down, until it ends up taking us over. Give the Devil a foot in the door and he destroys your whole life.

I tell my clients that addiction does not have to look like drugs and alcohol, although they are popular ones. We all have some addictions, some of the time. Sometimes they look impressive, like work or money. Sometimes addiction looks neutral, like Facebook or shopping or video games. Addiction is our favorite distraction, what we use to numb us so that we don't express our emotions around pain. Don't condemn or hate an addict. They are in a world of pain, even if they don't look like it, outwardly.

There are other ways our unexpressed pain plays out. Depression . . . that is not crying all the time. The definition of the word is to *press down*. It's an unconscious flattening of our lives when we don't feel anything because if we let it all out, we are terrified that we will lose control, that we would never be able to stop crying or raging. That we might end our own lives from the immensity of our inner torment. And we all know what panic and anxiety look like, when everything goes haywire. Sometimes one's body chemistry needs pharmaceutical help to do spiritual work, and sometimes people can manage independently. But it can't be gotten rid of without a journey inward.

"Don't you want to find someone you love who loves you back?" I asked Alejandra one day over the cards and a cup of coffee in Ana Sofia's office. "It's got to be a cold, empty life if it's only about stuff . . ."

"Eh, I don't believe in love," Alejandra said with all the drama of Greta Garbo. "I did that the first time, and it got me no-thing."

I didn't buy that. I think that she had been hurt, deeply. Alejandra had a heart in there somewhere. I knew it.

"David es a loser," Ana Sofia said to me in a tarot session, elaborating that he couldn't hold a job and did nothing but play video games. This explained his Page of Wands in reverse, which is immaturity. And yet it also came out that he helped her with her homework, kept up the house, and hoped, I think, that Ana Sofia would come home and spend some time with him again one day.

Ana Sofia wanted to have a baby. The Moon reversed showed that her biological clock was ticking, and her time was running out. For her, it didn't matter with whom she had it.

David's cards showed that he wanted to be a father with Ana Sofia and that he would be content to be a househusband. Sounded perfect from where I sat. Ana Sofia was not the maternal, stay-at-home type anyway. She would have her baby and be free to travel and keep her boyfriends.

But Ana Sofia had been pressing Marcus to marry her. Even with her fancy fifty-thousand-dollar engagement ring, Marcus wouldn't set a date.

"What es the problem?" Ana Sofia asked me, exasperated with him.

I looked at his cards, chuckling to myself. There was the Three of Pentacles reversed. Of course.

"Um, it's just that Marcus wants you to be divorced first."

Who needs cards? Anyone would know this.

She rolled her big, brown eyes as if Marcus was being irrationally difficult.

"Oh, thaaat . . ."

Details, details.

Over those last few sessions I had with Ana Sofia, the baby energy had shown up in the cards with great gusto: Ace of Cups reversed, the Fool reversed, Page of Cups reversed. Ana Sofia wanted a child and felt like it was the one thing she could not have. I told her this, and she nodded, saying nothing. I saw the Magician and the Hierophant.

"It looks like you'll be getting medical assistance for this if it happens."

She nodded again. "Alrrready we are doing it. Marcus gave a donation, but eet was no good. They tell me I'm fine. It's him. Will he be able? Or do I find someone else?"

The cards revealed that Marcus would be able to successfully produce healthy sperm to father a child *if* he kept at it. However, he also showed as not being all that interested. Marcus had already fathered a few children who were grown and nearly Ana Sofia's age. He was in his sixties now. Going out to give sperm samples was a magnanimous favor that he was doing for Ana Sofia around his busy work schedule.

"You can get pregnant with Marcus if Marcus will keep going. He'll need to donate at least three times. Any other questions?"

"Yes. Tell me about Garrry."

I saw the Hermit and the Emperor reversed. "Gary is too old for you and not very nice," I warned. Ana Sofia laughed and agreed that they were incompatible in every department. But he was rich, a surgeon, interested, and well, you know . . .

"Is there any *other* love coming?" It was the question that they both had for me after I looked at their lists of questions about the men they knew in the present.

Love? No, probably not love. But there were lots of men and money.

Personalities in the Tarot

As you become more comfortable with the tarot, people will begin to show up for you in the cards based on their personality description. You will personally also start to identify with a card or two. Generally, the Kings are masculine energy, and the Queens are feminine. My husband is inevitably the King of Pentacles: a fair, grounded man who is successful, responsible, and dependable. I am the Queen of Wands: a creative, energetic woman with an extreme passion for art, animals, and children. When I'm on top of my game, and especially in matters of intuition, I'm the High Priestess. As a mom, I'm the Empress. I am the Queen of Wands reversed when I am at my worst. Children and teenagers are all Pages. Young people (or immature grown people) are Knights. Gender doesn't apply to the lower-ranked court cards.

THE TOWER.

16
THE TOWER

Another high school lock-in: the ultimate adolescent babysitting party. Those insane evenings take too much out of me. Beginning at midnight and running until four in the morning, I feel hungover for days after working them, despite the fact I don't drink. I don't do late nights any longer. This exhausted misery is a sure fit for the Tower card, a card of collapse and the breaking out of old paradigms and systems. It's not all doom and gloom, but it's never easy.

The Tower's picture shows the black of night with male and female bodies flailing off a burning, crumbling structure. It's a busy card, with lightning, clouds, fire, and Hebraic *yod* marks, little yellow squiggles, representing the active dew of thought and what we create with our minds. Was this card really so different from a lock-in? The Tower may be the most feared of all the Major Arcana tarot cards. The Tower is about disruption and catastrophe at worst and re-creating at best. Whether it is right side up or reversed, this card tells the reader that the foundation for something is wrong, the structure of your life is falling apart, and that it's time to rebuild. We all face the Tower from time to time.

A band played Top 40 tunes inside the cavernous gym, where most of the kids congregated. The event organizers positioned us entertainers at different stations in the main hallway outside the gymnasium: the caricature guy stood at his easel with a felt-tip pen in hand, whipping out his exaggerations and flatteries in jet black ink on blinding white pages.

Someone did back and neck massages in a floor-facing chair. A henna tattoo artist made her mystical sienna mud designs on girls' hands, a face painter turned kids into animals and insects, and then there was me.

I wished I hadn't accepted this job. The throbbing music, the hyped-up, hormonal teenagers, the fluorescent lighting overhead . . . it was just too much so late at night. I knew that I was the old fogey cliché, but my inner voice reminded me that everything does happen for a reason, and I was supposed to be there for someone that evening. I would handle it, powered by the fuel given to me by my younger son Ross, who worked in a coffee shop back then and had hooked me up with an iced coffee, double-jolted with caffeine. I kept it behind the long curtains around my table, next to my purse on the floor, to help me get through this event and drive home safely as the sun came up.

The kids queued up in front of me, ready to be entertained. Most were girls wanting to know if so-and-so liked them or really, *really* liked them. It was the typical teenage stuff: they whispered boys' names followed by shrieks and giggles. Only a few boys visited my tarot table, preferring to crowd around the doorways, catching the girls as they passed in and out of the gym. The girls who sat down before me were all cute, stylish teens with chipped blue and green nail polish, transparent braces, and cat's eye eyeliner, picking at Rice Krispies treats and Chex Mix snacks the mothers had made, which they'd piled on Styrofoam plates at the buffet. Their energy was uncontained, their volume knob cranked to ten, and there wasn't a hint of sleepiness, despite the fact it was already past midnight.

Some tarot scholars consider the Tower to be the mythological Tower of Babel. The story goes that man got so full of himself, desiring to build a tower up to the same level as God. God assigned all the workers different languages to create confusion around the project and separate everyone around the world. This place sure was confusing, and the talk was deafening, everyone speaking and few listening. A couple of kids were forward-thinking enough to consider college and future careers. And then, there were those different kids, the ones who were not huddled up giggling in their cliques. The ones with maybe a bit of extra weight or acne. They stood in line too, and when it was their turn, they sat blank-eyed in front of me, waiting for their sentence. Waiting to see if I would pronounce them as loved or unlovable, as successes or failures.

That night, the kids didn't have to say much to me. The tarot cards voiced their hopes and fears, and I listened like a priest in a confessional as they came and left. In tarot readings, I don't always know what I've said or why it moves a person, but that doesn't matter. I see the slight tremors or the rosy flush across the chest and face and I know I have gotten through. I was called there that night for those kids to help them get through whatever struggles were going on, channel whatever Spirit intended for them, and maybe provide them a little bit of guidance.

I saw Elaine standing about three people down in the line. She waited for the cool girls ahead to finish. Elaine was a little plump, a little awkward, and clearly on her own at this event. As she reached up to tame a renegade strand of frizzy orange hair that was in her eyes, her long sleeve slid down for the briefest moment, and I saw a series of what appeared to be half-healed, self-inflicted cuts.

Effects of the Tower card come on suddenly. Like the flash of lightning in its picture, the Tower is a shock and creates upset, but the lightning can also be understood as a flash of revelation. Bodies fall from this building, and one has a crown, suggesting that adversity and trouble happen to those of high status and low. The Qabalah states that our experience of "suddenly" is not accurate. "Suddenly" is usually years of repressed consciousness building up. The lesson of the Tower, then, is to teach us that without a healthy outlet, the pressure will increase until something explodes.

Perhaps you will judge me now as a false tarot card reader for using my observation to guide my reading. I accept that I was meant to see Elaine's cuts because I am in this work to help people; I was divinely guided to get right to the point in my limited amount of time with her. I smiled and joked with the girls in front and told them about their romances, their dreams, and what they wanted to hear. And then Elaine sat down tentatively.

The cards never lie, and Elaine's revealed to us both her bitter truth. Her spread was all Swords. How appropriate. The Nine of Swords, the

Three of Swords, and the Five of Swords reversed. A lot of misery. I had to keep the line moving, so I gave it to her straight:

"Elaine, this Nine of Swords, it's such a fascinating card. Looks scary, right? This woman, she is crying alone in the dark. But don't judge the card from that. In the tarot, Swords are our thoughts. These nine swords on her wall are her thoughts and feelings. None of the swords are attacking her. And oh, look how she's turned away from them! She doesn't want to deal with her feelings, and that's why she is suffering. Her world is fine. See, she's even tucked cozily into her bed. Her anguish is inside."

Elaine nodded. Her full, freckled face shook ever so slightly. I could see the wisdom of the ages getting through to her. I thought about how our culture has been brainwashed to avoid discomfort at all costs, physically and mentally. This is why the use and abuse of opiates and antidepressants is so rampant. But Buddha and other mystics encourage us to go *into* the pain. The shaman goes into the desert or wilderness to do the inner work of confronting the self and any suffering he has carried along; he stays there to overcome it. There's a reason they call it "growing pains." Growing isn't easy, and we don't ever stop growing until we are done on this planet.

"This Three of Swords? Now, that's a concern," I said. "Look at it." I pointed to the giant bleeding heart with three swords running through it. "You *seek* pain. Increasing your pain is your goal. Maybe pain is what you go to, to hurt on the outside instead of the inside. Or maybe the pain is your comfort, to remind you that you are still here, even if the world seems to have forgotten."

There. I said it. I called Elaine out about what she was doing to herself.

The Tower is a card of blackness. It appears to be, and is, absolutely hopeless. The Tower's anguish serves as a function to warn us of danger, but when pain is chronic, that warning is useless. It's like one of those crazy car alarms that blasts on and on and on. People stop paying attention and try to ignore it or tune it out. There are twenty-two *yod* marks around the Tower in the picture, one mark for every card in the Major Arcana, explaining that our minds move us from one situation to another. The dew of thought affects everything.

"Elaine, we have all been taught to run from pain, physical or emotional. It's human nature. If we have been abused, traumatized, or victimized, we think it is wrong even to recognize that the hurt is there. As though acknowledging it will weaken us. Or else we are afraid that if we do let the upset out it will swallow us up, and we will stay in a place of victimhood and be depressed forever. Are you with me so far?"

She nodded. The kids in line fell back to give her a little more time with me. I don't know how, but they knew something consequential was going on.

"Elaine, if you're not living fully in the presence of what's happening, right now, no matter how terrible . . . if you're not understanding and expressing what is happening inside you in the current moment, you won't be able to think clearly to know what to do next . . . and you'll be tempted to keep hurting yourself to escape it all."

"But it's just . . ." She couldn't make herself continue. Not there, in school, with everyone around.

But I knew where she was going with this.

"Don't judge yourself by saying that some people have it worse, so you should get past your stuff. Sure, some people suffer more, but that doesn't mean you feel it less. I am trying to tell you that you are more likely to get out of your pain if you take the time to be aware that you are *in* it. And if you do not do this inner work, you will hurt yourself in a multitude of other ways. Your body and mind will create other problems as a sign for you to stop and notice their root cause. Does that make sense?"

A tear rolled down her cheek. She sat there in silence, her eyes locked into mine.

It's a gamble when I call someone out on their behavior or if I suggest a path for them. They might not be ready. I can't fix anyone. I can't make someone face what they don't want to face. And who wants to face the Tower? The Tower says that life as you formerly knew it is no more, and you can't go on living as you were. Some tarot readers interpret the Tower as a card of imprisonment, like Rapunzel in the fairy tales. However you spin it, the Tower isn't comfortable.

Tears ran down Elaine's cheeks. The emotion had begun to well up in me too, and my voice cracked a little as I continued. Elaine was accomplishing her terrible goal of self-destruction, but hers was a no-win situation.

"Now, see this Five of Swords? This means life is a fight. But in reverse, as you have it, the fight is with yourself. Elaine, you're beating yourself up. You hurt yourself outside because you don't want to look at the inside emotions. But here's the thing: the way to healing is *feeling*. It is about experiencing that pain on the *inside*, not on the outside. I know that expressing and living in the place of your emotional stress is the last thing you want to do. But if you allow yourself to go to that dark and awful place and fully engage with it, it will stop controlling you. You've been trying to distract yourself, hurting yourself with all those Swords, right? It doesn't work so well, does it? No, you *have* to get the feelings out. Drop your judgment about trying to be stronger or to just get over it. You might have to get a counselor. Maybe you can talk to a best friend. Journaling and having a good cry can help. Maybe all of that. But you've got to let this stress out because you will eventually destroy yourself if you don't. Do you understand? Do you know how serious this is?"

She nodded again, almost mute and in shock that I would say this.

"I'm going to pull one last card for you," I said. I pulled Judgement in reverse.

"This is a card of Judgement Day. It's about being rewarded for good behavior or punished for your sins. You, with Judgement in reverse, punish yourself. It's time to stop that. You're done. You were put on this Earth to be a gift and make a difference. Decide right now to start living for positive reasons. Decide to make this world a better place."

I had to move on to the next person. I was as wrung out as she was. I stood up and held her hands. "Promise me you'll be kinder to yourself?"

Oh, high school. It's so tough, even for the most blessed of kids. I looked at those endless rows of towering red and gray steel lockers lining the hallways. The waxed wood floor of the gymnasium was just in my view through the open double steel doors. The same loudspeakers, class bells, and fire sprinklers from my day, mounted at the juncture of the walls and ceiling, now had the additional company of security cameras. Some schools had installed metal detectors, and students' backpacks and purses had to be plastic and see-through. But for all this prevention, were students really secure?

The card that follows the Tower in the Major Arcana is the Star. The Star features a winsome young maiden bearing all her perfect skin to God and the world. She is sometimes recognized as Pandora, who broke the rules and let the demons out of the box, making a mess of everything. But one encouraging sprite, Hope, remained.

"I promise," she said in a tiny voice.

I hugged her, and she slipped away into the crowd of teens and thumping music as another girl slid into her place, ready for a reading. I can only hope that Elaine kept her promise. Her life depended upon it.

What about When You See Something Terrible Ahead?

People ask me this question all the time. I believe that I can read my clients'—and anyone's—cards because we are connected, just by being alive. I show my clients what they already know on a subconscious level. It's somewhat like dream analysis, except for that fascinating question: *How do the right cards show up in the correct position to give us the answers or tell the story?* That's the magic part because we're connected through the life force, which I call *God*, but you may call it *Source* or *Universal Energy*, or another term. Just by being alive, we are hooked into it. We are children of God, and so we have the power to change things if we want to own that power. But what did the story of Spiderman tell us? *With power comes great responsibility.* I encourage my clients to own the circumstances of their lives, good and bad. We mystics believe that we are all at least half in control of everything happening to us at all times.

17

THE STAR

"I have a theory," my then twenty-one-year-old son, Ross, declared. "All the on-the-fringe kids from high school are here, and now, I am one of them."

Ross helped me get my tent in order for another day's work at the St. Louis Renaissance Festival. Ah, the Ren Fest! It is a time when grown adults acquire false British and French accents, dress in suits of armor and jester outfits, or as ladies of the medieval court and beggars.

The cannon down by the entrance gate sounded its great boom, announcing that the doors were open. It was already hot at 10:00 a.m. that Memorial Day weekend, even as the rain still came down. Everything was steamy and damp. Ross looked handsome in his puffy ivory poet blouse, which he hated—but I had paid him to help me out, and the dress code was strict. He could use the money, and I enjoyed his company. We both decided, rules be damned, that we were not faking accents. I had to tune in to Spirit. I couldn't bother with that acting crap.

The Star card is ruled by the sign of Aquarius and features a lovely naked maiden pouring water from pitchers onto land and in the water. Our land and water boundaries were a chore to define at the Renaissance Festival, as the park was part flooded from spring rains, and the plywood platforms on which our tents were erected collected pools of it. Water in the tarot symbolizes love, emotion, fertility, cleansing, healing, and the elixir of life. The seven stars on the Star card refer to the Pleiades, which rise into the skies in our festival month of May.

The Renaissance Festival had been in full swing for a couple of weeks. It is the most challenging tarot work that I have done, physically and spiritually. Physically, I had to move and set up my tent and furniture in this forested park, hang signs and decorations, and work long hours in the elements. Those late-spring May dates meant we faced it all: cold snaps, summer thunderstorms, pollen, flooding, and then the blazing St. Louis heat and humidity. At the end of the eight-hour day, I would emerge hungry, thirsty, and stiff from the almost constant sitting to accommodate the long lines of people, soaked in perspiration, asthmatic, and covered in mosquito bites. I would have to pee, but the idea of those overused porta potties in the heat was too horrid to endure unless absolutely necessary. I would typically lose most or all of my voice due to so much talking. My last Ren Fest was in 2016 after which I wound up in the emergency room with a pulmonary embolism.

It's a living.

Spiritually, the work was not that proverbial "walk in the park," either. The massive crowds meant that I experienced radical changes in energy from one person to the next, trying to connect on a deep level yet keeping each reading under ten minutes. I had to be brief yet leave them with something resonant and meaningful.

I refused to remove the plastic sheeting that covered my handmade burlap and cloth signs until the rain ended. I knew plastic was not very Renaissance, nor was the stepladder in my tent, but I would soon need it, and I didn't want to get muddier than I already was. Behind the silken veils of my tent and kept out of sight, I hid a multitude of modern-day gadgets: a thermos of coffee and a cooler with snacks, a cellphone charger, phone, and aerosol bug repellant. Ross and I rolled up the sides of the tent and lifted the curtains so they did not wick up the pools of rainwater remaining on the wooden floor. I wore a long multi-colored peasant skirt that was already soaked at its hem and growing heavy.

The first hour was usually slow. It took a while for the customers to get their bearings and plan out what areas they wanted to visit and how they wanted to spend their money. They worked their paths from the entrance back to my setup in the politically incorrect "Gypsy Camp" area of the woods, across from the petting zoo and next door to the Drunken Parrot Pub. A woman dressed like a wench who worked the beer tap took advantage of the quiet moment and dropped by my tent to chat.

"As I stood in line at the 'privy,'" she said, "I listened to doubters who laughed at what you do. I said, 'I suggest you wait in line. You won't be disappointed.' I hadn't realized it at the time, Julia, but yesterday you brought me a message straight from God."

"Oh? I'm so glad!" I said, giving her a quick hug. Of course, I didn't recall a thing about the reading. They flit in and out of my head like dreams. But there was no time to chat much longer. Customers were coming.

Like the Star card, people come to me at the Renaissance Festival for hope. With these crowds of people, there are often similar stories and themes. A story of hope that I have seen manifest numerous times in my profession is regarding fertility matters.

The young married couple took their seats in my tarot tent amid the flowing pink and purple satin curtains that make up my walls when it is not raining. They both appeared to be in their early thirties. The wife was Mexican American, and he was of Scotch-Irish descent, announcing his heritage by wearing a tartan kilt.

"I play the bagpipes too!" he said proudly. "Although I don't know if they'd want me to bring it here."

"They would have loved it," I laughed, getting their names, Owen and Carmelita, as I laid down their cards. Their first card was the Empress in reverse. The woman on the Empress card is often considered to be Venus/Aphrodite, or Persephone, daughter of Demeter, the Great Mother. But in reverse, there are troubles regarding motherhood.

"You're struggling to have a baby," I said. This is a common problem; I see it for clients at least once a week. They both nodded with solemnity.

"What if it never happens? It has been over a year of trying," Owen asked. Couples dealing with infertility continually ask this question, the worst possible scenario, upon which they remain fixated.

"Do you see what you're doing with your energy?" I said back. "Your focus is on it *not* happening. You're a child of God, and your mind is powerful. When you're in the car behind the wheel, what you're looking at is where you're driving to, right? You're driving to this baby *not* happening with your focus on fear. Put your focus on what you want, not what you don't want."

"But I'm scared," Carmelita said. "What if I'm disappointed?"

"You're already disappointed. Fear closes up your conducive energy. Being fearful of your fear, even more so. Think of it like this: An athlete keeps his eyes on the prize. He does not say, 'What if I trip and fall? What if I don't make it to the finish line?' Because that opens up space for what he doesn't want to happen. You can't get any-where if you don't embrace first that it is possible."

I saw my words begin to make sense to them. There was a bright-ness in their eyes, if not in the expression on their faces. And beside that Empress reversed was the Star card.

The Star card shows the water of spring rains bringing flowers from the ground. The Star brings harmony and a sense of well-being. The characteristics associated with the Star are renewed energy, inspi-ration, and healing. These give hope and a cheerful outlook, to man-ifest what is possible. Owen and Carmelita began to see how their actions, obsessing over not having a baby, had gotten in the way.

"Have you ever met a couple who gave up on having children of their own, adopted, and then got pregnant? It happens all the time. The pressure is off, and they relax and quit all the negative energy. But let's not wait until that happens. You have to believe now. Consider this: Thomas Edison failed at making the light bulb something like ten thousand times. Anyone else would have said, 'Give it up, dude.

It's not possible.' But he knew in the core of his being that it could happen, and so it did. Do you honestly think he would have kept trying if he did not believe it would happen?"

Carmelita said, "It's just that . . . I don't know how to believe it. I am so alone in this. Like I'm the only one in the world who can't . . .'" She dabbed at her eyes with a tissue.

"Stop it!" her husband corrected her, getting the gist of what I had said. "You're reinforcing the negative. Right, Julia?"

"Right," I smiled. "Fast learner. Let me give you both some homework, but this is most important for Carmelita. I want you to meditate every day, focusing on how wonderful it will be to hold that precious newborn baby in your arms. I want you to think of kissing its soft skin and savor the weight and warmth of your baby as it suckles at your breast."

To get so detailed and personal felt terrifying to Carmelita. More tears flowed.

"But I'm afraid!"

In the picture on the Star card, the jug of water poured onto land turns into five rivulets. These symbolize the elements from which all life is created. They may be interpreted either in Western fashion as earth, fire, water, air, and spirit, or in the Eastern manner of wood, fire, earth, metal, and water. Whichever doctrine you prefer, the belief is that from these elements comes all of creation.

"Of course you are. But you will do it anyway because you are doing an exceptional job of creating the opposite right now. It can't—won't—happen if you accept the opposite. Realizing this dream is more than merely picturing it. You have to feel into it. Like a memory that hasn't happened yet. Can you practice that?"

They nodded. There is a bird in a tree in the background of the Star card. This bird is considered to be an ibis, the bird of fertility. A year later, I received an email that Owen and Carmelita were blissfully pregnant and expecting a little girl in a month. As soon as we destroy the fear and negativity that we accidentally invite in, nurture, and even defend as it terrorizes our minds, we can all make our miracles.

★

Over the years, I have done many readings on the topic of health at the Ren Fest, but none stayed with me more than this one for a boy and his mother:

Kyle was eleven or twelve and already fully, proudly aware that he was gay. He smiled broadly and plopped his pink satin shorts down on a chair in the tent as his mom took the other seat. She shook my hand and introduced herself as Suzie.

"Love your tent!" Kyle said of the pink and purple satin walls billowing in the wind. "What do *you* see for *me?*" he said, pointing his finger at me and then himself, making it a game. He was dramatic, adopting a playful affectation. I loved how this kid loved himself and his life.

Kyle had a lot of strong Major Arcana cards. The Sun, which I saw as a kind of a spotlight on him; the Chariot, which is movement; and most excitingly, the Star. The Star is often also seen as a card for vision and aspiration, a star to hitch one's wagon to, as the idiom goes.

"Kyle, I see you attaining a hope or a dream. You could be a celebrity in your field."

Kyle jumped up, shouting, "Yaaay!" and his mother burst into tears.

"Really?" she dared to ask. After a second, she composed herself and explained.

"You see, Kyle was born with cerebral palsy. But all he's ever wanted to do is be a dancer, since he was three years old. He's quite good, and he works through it. He won't take no for an answer."

"Suzie, I know nothing about cerebral palsy. But I know from his cards that Kyle is a talented dancer, that he will be great, and one day the world will know him. The Star is seen globally. Believe in him as he believes in himself. He's got this. He knows what he has to do."

I then shared a story with them of another Star card I read for a young man I have known since he was five. His band toured through our town in their own van, and they shacked up on the floors and sofas at my house, doing it all hardscrabble and on their own. I pulled the Star card for my young friend, and today he is a multiplatinum recording artist. Some people are natural-born stars.

Suzie and Kyle gave each other celebratory hugs, and then they both hugged me.

As much as I adored him, I was glad to get an underage kid out of my tent as the action at the pub next door cranked up, my silk curtains a poor barrier to its booming volume. It was a full-on party over there. In his pirate cap and false eye patch, the jovial bartender Ed got progressively more drunk as the day went on, telling long rambling stories and jokes, fully in his element. Most of the Ren Fest workers lived for that time of the year when they could dress up and pretend there was no nine-to-five in their walled-in, protected world of white horses and knights.

And there was that particular crowd of women, er, *wenches,* who liked to dress up in their tight corsets with bosoms heaving, get drunk on the cheap beer they guzzled from plastic horns and steins, and see whose attention they might elicit on that sweaty summer day in a public park. The Ren Fest permitted them to show all they've got, and they weren't shy about it. I heard the stories of swinging after-show sex parties and couples stepping outside the fairgrounds, heading further into the woods to see what kind of fun might be had under a voluminous skirt.

I had a long line of people at my tent's entrance, but it was hard to concentrate on my cards without listening to the come-ons of the Marine-turned-dance instructor dressed as a dashing pirate with knee-high leather boots and a swashbuckling sword next door. He was his own kind of Star on this smaller stage.

"The woman needs to know very little about the dance," he explained to the rapt ladies who encircled him. "It is the man's job to lead her, to show her off. To display her as an elegant rose."

I could hear him then, demonstrating steps. "One-two-and-one-two . . ." Taking various women by the hand. I'm sure that bedswerver charmed many a strumpet that night.

Sometimes it is not my job to give the Star card's hope to a client. Sometimes, my job is to make a correction. Because of the nature of my work, and maybe especially in the Ren Fest setting, some people assume me to be a full-on witch, practicing black magic or the darker forms of the occult. I'll get people all the time asking for spells, and I will respond with, "Why do you want to manipulate others?" One year, I made up my own fake spells for sale at the Ren Fest, but the candles melted in the hot sun and the would-be buyers soon figured out that I had sneakily tried to indoctrinate them to use their own God power with *A Course in Miracles* meditations rather than to coast on the lazy ways of Satan.

Do I acknowledge the existence of dark power? Sure, to a point. It can't hurt me because, as Marianne Williamson says, the Devil is all in your head—but that's the worst place he could possibly be. The Star in reverse can be read as a card of deception. The Star is so captivating that we think, *how can she represent anything undesirable?* But the opposite of hope is hopelessness. Remembering that the woman in the picture is Persephone, who was tricked by Hades to go to the Underworld for a season every year, when nothing grew and days were cold, short, and dark.

This particular afternoon had grown hot. The promised sun finally lit silver linings in the cloudy sky. My wind chimes hung still, limp and silent. Ross once again rolled up all four of my walls and tied back the curtains, hoping for a nonexistent breeze to flow through. Two large young men came into my tent next. They were about nineteen or twenty years old, both dressed in black goth clothes from head to toe, with black eyeliner, piercings, and devilish tattoos, looking about as far from the Renaissance as possible. Their aim was snarky rebellion. As my background is in the music industry, their fashion style was no big deal to me and nothing to cast judgment over—I enjoy the Cure and Nine Inch Nails with the best of them.

The larger of the two young men spoke first. The three hundred pounds of him (if I were going to guess) took up most of the space in front of my table, impossible to ignore.

"So, like, what kind of occult do you do? Do you mess with demons, do séances, or cast spells and cool shit like that?"

I chuckled. "Um, sorry. Just boring old tarot cards. I live in the light. What's your name?"

"Danny," he said. I never got the name of his friend.

"What's the point, then?" Danny asked. His friend still stood outside the doorway in the hot sun, listening in.

"Tarot is about showing you where your energy is going. It gives you tools to understand yourself and guidance to make the changes you want."

The ibis, the bird on the Star card is the bird of the Egyptian god Thoth, the god of wisdom. The ibis eats poisonous cobras and symbolizes that man is protected and saved by his wits. I said a quick prayer of protection, as these boys were dark energy.

Danny slumped into one of my folding chairs, pulled out a twenty, and said, "I guess I'll try it."

On the Star card, Persephone stands upon the water, showing the occasional impossible nature of hope. The Lovers card in reverse showed worry around Danny's love life, but that's pretty normal for young people. I put down the next card, and before I could say anything, Danny laughed and pointed it out to his friend and said, "Excellent!" It was the Devil in reverse, a card that showed addiction, depression, and anxiety. *Not* excellent.

Both Temperance reversed and the Moon in reverse showed Danny was in less than ideal physical condition, charging toward self-annihilation. And then, his last card: the Star in reverse. While the Star is usually seen as heartening, if it doesn't have the support of other cards showing real action, it's a loss. It's somewhat like the Seven of Cups, a card I call "the bucket list." The Star in reverse is empty and futile because what use is a dream if no effort is put forth to make it happen? I began to explain each card to Danny as diplomatically as I could.

"Here's the thing about the Devil," I warned them both since his friend had edged into the tent to hear better and get into the shade. "When you let the darkness in, he takes you over. You don't think there is a price tag for messing with evil? You may get your little bits of power now and then. But it will be at the expense of your physical body, your world success, and your soul. Those who seek power in the dark side are never well or happy. They are usually either obese"—I tried to look in his eyes and say this as a matter of fact; I wasn't criticizing him—"or they're emaciated. They get diseases and terrible depression, and a lot of addiction problems. And addiction doesn't have to look like drugs and alcohol. Sometimes it can look like relationships or video games."

Danny cast a knowing glance over at his friend.

"Addiction is the thing you do to avoid true living. It's the thing you do to destroy yourself so that your dreams will never come true because you identify with troubles more. You don't want to feel that distress, and at the same time, you won't let go of it."

Outside my tent, two displaced, dazed, probably drunken harlequins looked like butterflies lost in a dizzy, directionless flapping dance. The heat had gotten to them. They cavorted toward the mud draining along the sides of the path, their little satin boots sinking in. They were happy for the bit of coolness on their feet without considering the long-term damage to their outfits. I thought about how adolescence is like a perpetual chrysalis. So many want to stay there and never dare to stretch their wings.

In some tarot decks, that ibis on the Star card is replaced with a butterfly. Maybe you have heard about how the *imaginal cells* carry the genetic information of the butterfly. The caterpillar dies into the butterfly. He becomes a gooey soup from which the imaginal cells take over, and a butterfly grows. That caterpillar doesn't have to know or remember anything to self-actualize as a butterfly. It's his job to fall apart, like in the Tower card. When we hold ourselves in addiction and paralysis, we never face the scary stuff, and so we never grow, and nothing good happens to us—we will always be the caterpillar, or worse yet, the goo.

"I'm hoping you will get smart and get your shit together. Both of you. Until then, I don't hold out a lot of hope."

Danny stood up and bellowed to his friend, "Did she really just say that to me?" The friend remained silent in the doorway, now smirking. "Did she pretty much just tell me that I'm doomed to be a no-success, sick, unloved loser?"

I sat on my side of the table and looked him in the eye.

"Did you want me to lie to you, Danny?"

I would not take it back. I wanted to see these young men do something worthwhile with their lives, for themselves, and for the world. To quit living in that in-between caterpillar place wearing their fake painted faces. These boys could be of value. Everyone can, as soon as they can conceive of this idea as true. They could grow wings. They could reclaim their God selves, which would be waiting for them when they finally grew up and figured it out. But until then, they lumbered out of my tent, laughing in my direction.

I took a hit from my asthma inhaler, and my hands began to shake from the rush of albuterol. I was done for the day and nearly done for the season. I told myself that it wouldn't be too soon if I never saw another porta potty. And then, the Renaissance Festival cannon sounded that it was the closing time of 6 p.m., the clouds grew darker, and a refreshing wind came with a sprinkle of rain to rinse away the residue of the day and give us hope for tomorrow.

Is Tarot Evil?

Some of my friends are very Christian and uncomfortable with tarot. While I respect anyone's decision to avoid spirituality that makes one uneasy, I'd like to explain a few things:

Tarot does not call spirits, good or evil, into play. Tarot isn't a Ouija board, a séance, or even prophecy. The idea behind the tarot is that we all have access to that knowledge and power because we are all one, of one spirit (which I call God). We are wiser and more in tune with ourselves and others than we consciously comprehend. The tarot is just a tool to tune in to this knowledge.

As a reminder, what the tarot shows us about the future is not fixed. We always have the power to change our path through the decisions that we make.

18
THE MOON

It was a quiet summer afternoon when a young girl called me from a phone number on the Illinois side. The Mississippi River cuts the border between Missouri and St. Louis, as a river cuts through the center of the Moon tarot card. To the west is Missouri and the city of St. Louis. To the east, in Illinois, is East St. Louis, an abject, rough, industrial area of abandoned factories and warehouses, pawnshops, and strip clubs. East St. Louis is a city to drive around or past, but not through.

"Can you tell me what's wrong with my grandpa?" the girl asked me in a small voice. "He is having chest pains, and he can't feel anything in his left hand."

Oh, shit. She didn't want a reading. She wanted magic. She wanted an instant diagnosis and advice to fix her grandfather at that very moment.

The Moon is a card of physical and mental health and sometimes the changeability of hormonal situations or chemical imbalances. If you look up in the sky, the moon is in a different place every day. It is ever-changing. Sometimes it's waxing, sometimes waning, sometimes full and bright, and sometimes not there at all.

In the background on the phone, I heard a man yell out to her in a panic. "Did you get her on the phone yet?"

"Yes," the girl shouted back to him. "I'm talking to her now." I could tell that she was trying to keep her composure and be mature, but I'd guess she was maybe twelve or thirteen. She was scared.

Sometimes the Moon is a card of the feminine, as the moon has a twenty-eight-day cycle, like the female menses. In the picture on the tarot card, the Moon is shown in three phases, echoing the three phases of femininity or the triple goddess imagery of Isis as maiden, mother, and crone. Because of these three phases, the Moon card often represents the times of puberty, fertility, and menopause. The girl was the Moon waxing, and I was the Moon waning, trying to help her.

"Honey," I said in my most motherly voice, "You need to get your grandpa to a doctor right away. I am not a doctor, but I know this is bad. He can't rest through this until he's better. Is there someone who can drive him? Can you call 911?"

There was a long pause. She hadn't expected my answer. She wanted a quick piece of advice to fix everything or reassurance that he would be fine. She didn't want to go against the wishes of her grandfather. The Moon reflects.

"Um, OK," she said, sounding confused. She hung up the phone.

We take institutions like 911 and the hospital emergency room for granted in the wealthier suburbs of St. Louis County. Judging from the phone number's area code, this man was probably Black, poor, and afraid to go to the ER for fear of how much it would cost. I wanted to cry.

Because the Moon is ever-changing, confusion is the name of the game with this card. It is a watery card of uncertainty, ruled by the tamed dog of consciousness and the wild wolf of the subconscious. The two are divided by a river leading to the Mother Sea, from which everything evolved. Mystic leaders such as Neville Goddard affirm that the female symbolizes the subconscious mind. This is why men, the tamed consciousness, are deemed the rulers in the Bible. However, nothing is created without a union of both minds.

Our subconscious mind, what we believe deep down, drives the direction of our lives. Suppose, for example, that we don't consider ourselves lovable or envision that we will ever be a success. In that case, those negative core beliefs are what will manifest despite our efforts to

conquer our problems. This fact created the multibillion-dollar industry of psychoanalysis.

The moon has been used to keep time since primitive man began
to mark the new and full moons. All of our beliefs are from past experiences, but that past is over and will never happen again. There is
another option if we can escape our beliefs, but it is hard to imagine
what we have never experienced. The Moon is often viewed as a card
of imagination and beliefs. What did this man believe? His past experience told him he had no options, so he shouldn't even try beyond his
sad appeal to me. My gut told me this man was in trouble, but like that
young girl, I was lost as to what I could do. I sat at home in my office,
alternating between prayer and trying to figure out how I could help, if
I could help at all.

Fifteen minutes later, the man himself called me.

"Miz Julia, I need your help. I'm all hurting, and, and it's like a car
fell on me . . . It's like I can't get my breath. . . ."

He sounded elderly and disoriented.

"Mam, I need to know what's wrong," he continued. "My hand and
my arm . . . I can't feel anything, and I can't make them work."

"Sir, this could be very serious, and these might be signs of a heart
attack or a stroke. You've *got* to see a doctor. A psychic can't help you.
Do you understand? You need a physical doctor to look at your body
and make sure you're OK."

He told me that ambulances didn't come to his part of St. Louis
and hung up, but he called me back again in a few minutes.

"Can you do something to help with the pain? I can't take the pain."

In mysticism, we often believe that we suffer physical ailments that
are symbolic, metaphors for what troubles us emotionally. Disease is disease. The Moon card has fifteen Hebraic *yod* symbols, fifteen, matching
the Devil card's number and the material world. Yods are the dew of
thought that nourish the ground of manifestation. Our thoughts create our realities. The spiritual mentor Louise Hay saw that everything
physical was a metaphor for emotional and spiritual issues, and there
are some interesting correlations. Cancer is deep hurt or anger eating

a person from the inside out. Foot trouble, which has plagued me for decades, is about being afraid to step forward. And heart attacks? Hay directly related these not to a lack of love but to a joyless life with worries over money.*

Tarot shows physical problems too, but this man's situation was too dire to waste time putting cards down. If I had done so, the heart trouble card is usually represented by the Three of Swords. Once, I watched a tarot reader announce that someone had back problems—she saw it from a card that had none of the usual symbolism for physical attributes. She showed me how, in that particular deck design, the swords were stacked in a way that reminded her of vertebrae. Simple as that. She followed her intuition. We see stories in the cards, and we see stories in our bodies. This is how we read.

You can't count on the Moon to be fully present as it mechanically moves through its synchronized rotations. This unfortunate man was obviously loved by his granddaughter, but was being failed by a system to care for his basic needs; a system, corporation, or government cannot love people. Only people can do that. I believe that we have to find our answers to these problems outside of government, which continues to fail us. But that, of course, requires individual effort, and most prefer to be uninvolved. Most people choose to only orbit from the outside, like the Moon, watching from its distance and never touching the problems of the world.

Again, I told the man that this is an emergency. This could be life-threatening. He kept asking the same questions: "Am I gonna be all right? Can you take away the pain?"

"Sir, will you give me your name and address?"

"Oh, Miz, nobody's gonna do nothin' about me." Then, he hung up.

I held my phone in my hand for a moment, as unsure as his young helper had been. Then I dialed 911 and asked if they would connect me to the police on the Illinois side.

---

*Louise Hay, *Heal Your Body: The Mental Causes for Physical Illness and the Metaphysical Way to Overcome Them* (Carlsbad, Calif.: Hay House, 1988), 39.

I soon understood why he had no faith in them. He was just another name on a long list. In her dull, moonish cycle of calls, the woman who took my information was more interested in *my* middle initial and birth date than in rushing to trace his number and find him. Exasperating. I barked out the details she wanted and hung up on her. Damn it. A man would die because she was more interested in my middle initial than in helping him.

The lobster crawling out of the ocean pictured on the Moon card represents our base animal nature and the lower mind. The Moon, at best, can only reflect on circumstances and dream in its darkness toward higher principles. Some say that the Moon hides the awareness that we are all one. When will we awaken? In mysticism we believe that this world is all illusion, all imagined like the Moon card's dreaminess, with only a shadow of reality. There is a higher path pictured on this card that separates the states of mind, conscious and subconscious. The trail winds far over the land, up into mountains and the unknown, past failing human bodies and all of our faulty institutions, past East St. Louis, beyond this frightening everyday reality of our projections.

As the moon waxes and wanes, its cycle repeats again and again.

The darkest side of the Moon card may represent schizophrenia and other forms of mental illness. Like those who suffer from these conditions, the Moon is unfailingly in our orbit but still not within reach. It circles the world as an outsider, beaming its false glow, an ersatz source of light. But its light is just a reflection, of course. That's why the Moon card may be interpreted as deception. And the worst lie is when one questions reality. After all, we get the word *lunacy* from *lunar*.

Scott and Frederick met up with me at a coffee shop in the Loop, a hip part of St. Louis's University City, around the prestigious and expensive Washington University. The two guys were nice-looking indie types in their late twenties; Scott sported a beard and flannel, even though we were well into June, and his friend Frederick was clean-shaven, wore a more appropriate t-shirt, and looked much younger than his years. Frederick had seen me before, and, as he put it to Scott, I was worth the chunk of change it cost to get direction from someone with spiritual knowledge.

We sat upstairs at a wooden table in the loft area, away from the commotion of the street traffic and those standing at the counter.

"Thanks for meeting me so quickly. I've been very stressed out. See, I'm having spiritual experiences," Scott said, leaning toward me, looking me in the eyes, and getting right to the point. "I'm hearing things and having visions, and I need to understand more about this because everything is crazy and falling apart right now. I lost my girlfriend and my job over it." Scott blew at the top of a mug of scalding-hot black coffee, stirring in packet after packet of sugar, round and round.

Concert and event fliers papered the walls around us, competing for our attention and vying to fill an entire calendar of weekend evenings: Tool with Melt Banana at the Scottrade Center. Sex Robots, Teenage Rehab, and the Humanoids at Off-Broadway. Funeral for a Friend at Creepy Crawl. The *Dog Days of Summer* concert lineup at Blueberry Hill's Duck Room across the street.

Dogs like those on the Moon card are linked with Greek moon goddesses, Egyptian Anubis, and Hades and the Underworld, and in medieval times they believed dogs could see the Angel of Death. And lest we not forget the howl of the wolf at the moon, which evokes our most primitive fears. The dog and the wolf pictured on the card defend the boundaries of waking and sleeping and of the spiritual and physical worlds. The wolf will occasionally send intuitive messages to the other side but should never fully cross into the dog's world, or there will be problems.

"I thought you'd be the right person to help him," Frederick cut in. "Because you won't judge, and you're kind. Scott has been laughed at by people he's trusted to share his experiences." Frederick nursed an iced tea, playing with it more than actually taking a drink.

"I promise that I won't laugh at you," I said, meaning it and raising my latte as a kind of gesture of solidarity. As a practitioner of mysticism, I have had dreams and visions myself and even heard voices, inner and audible. I'm not someone who judges, believing that anyone who sees or hears things should be condemned as crazy. But these things usually happen under particular circumstances, such as in the context of meditation or when I'm searching for an answer and channeling Spirit.

"Tell me what is going on, Scott."

"I get messages from my TV. . . ."

At that moment, I was transported in memory to several years earlier when I was in Bloomington, Indiana, researching in the Sylvia Plath archives. I had spent an eight-hour day reading her childhood journals and wanted to skip ahead to her young adult stuff, which felt far more interesting. But I needed to finish that 1945 journal, didn't I? Just to get it done? In my hotel room, I asked Sylvia out loud, "Sylvia, should I jump ahead or finish 1945?" Almost immediately, on the television I'd had on for background, an ad for a World War II movie lit up the room, and the announcer boomed out, "1945." I got my sign. And the next day, I found a transformative bit of information for my work. So, no. I wasn't bailing on Scott yet. I kept all of this to myself.

"What kind of messages?" I asked.

"Well," Scott said, "there is only one channel that I am allowed to watch."

"Allowed?" I said, beginning to get uneasy. This wasn't sitting right with me.

A couple of college kids clomped up the stairs and pulled up chairs at the table next to us. Scott lowered his voice.

"Yeah, this channel tells me what to do that day, what to say, even what to wear and eat. And it's spiritual. I know that. This is a God thing, unless it's a demon. I don't know. I haven't totally figured it out. But I have to do what it says. Believe me, Julia. I've heard all the *Poltergeist* and *Son of Sam* jokes, but I'm being real. Sober as a judge. I don't understand what it wants from me. But it's calling me, and I have to answer. This is my purpose."

The Moon is a card of illusion, delusion, fantasy, and spells. In the order of the tarot's Major Arcana, it precedes the Sun card, as initiates in the ancient mystery religions worked in darkness to gain enlightenment. Sometimes enlightenment is not to be found. Sometimes, like with Scott, the illusion and fantasy take over, and the actual world of reality is lost, intermittently or entirely.

My heart hurt for him. I didn't want to say what I had to tell him.

"Here's the thing, Scott. If your television is commanding you like that, if you don't have the power to turn it off or change the channel, that is not of God. God doesn't work like that. God is love. God only wants a higher purpose, and you always, always have free will."

Both Scott and Frederick looked down toward the floor, seeming disappointed.

"Damn," Scott said. "I had hoped you would say I was a prophet or visionary. But you think I'm sick? Crazy?"

"I can't diagnose any such thing. A doctor has to do that. But I have my concerns, and I want to know you're going to be all right. Will you go see a doctor? I know that is much less appealing than being the next Moses or Nostradamus."

The Moon is passive and wants things to flow without effort, like dreams.

"Dude," Scott said to Frederick, or maybe both of us, "I expected good news. I don't want to have to hide a problem and take medication. I like living in the occult world, and I like having this special . . . gift . . . and knowledge. I don't know that I want to let it go, you know? I have powers!"

I thought of my friend Matthew then, a person with schizophrenia on medication, who told me that demons commanded him to jump out of a third-story window. He did and survived, albeit with many broken bones, and was institutionalized after running into St. Louis Cathedral and begging for an exorcism. In schizophrenia the spirit world often turns very frightening.

Scott liked the mystery and potential acclaim these visions and insights might bring him one day if he were right and I was wrong. He liked the idea that he could be famous as an artist or a poet or have followers as a spiritual leader. But these things all slip into that all-consuming, greedy territory of ego, which is not of God either. We all want to matter. We forget that we do already, just by being here.

And so I said my goodbye, put my tarot cards back in the case, and walked outside into the increasingly warm city afternoon, hoping Scott would get the help he needs and wondering what the spirits might whisper in his ear about me as I journeyed home.

Reading for Those You Know, versus Reading for Strangers

When we read for our friends and family, we have to be careful about wanting to influence the reading. If we care too much, we get into that dangerous territory of bias and wanting the dreams of our loved ones to happen. But it might not be the right time for them, or they may have some major personal work to accomplish first. We, as tarot card readers, cannot get attached to timetables for dreams to come true.

I am happy to read for family and friends about casual things, but I usually read less well if a question involves their safety, financial security, or general happiness since I care deeply about them. For example, I have no problem looking into the success of my son's band going on tour in Europe. But if he asks me, "Will I be safe in Europe?" or even, "Will I make enough money to be able to pay my bills?" I can't go there. I'm too emotionally involved.

There is nothing more fun to a tarot reader than reading for strangers. It's a blank slate—you have no background or knowledge on them whatsoever and it's just pure reflection and intuition. These are often the best readings, and I have had many cry with emotion, hug me, and tell me how amazing I am. To which I just say, "It's not me. You're just seeing what you already know. You could do it too."

THE SUN .

19
THE SUN

The email came in through my website and began with these words: *I just wanted to reach out to you and let you know how your work has touched and influenced my life.*

The Sun, in general, is considered to be a cheery card in the Major Arcana. It is vibrant energy, joy, enlightenment, and celebration. Sometimes it has more subtle meanings, such as shining light on a situation.

I sometimes receive thank-you notes from clients who tell me that some insight or advice given to them in a tarot card reading has made a real difference. Blame it on my ego, I guess, because I naively thought, for a minute, that this email was going to go like that. As I read further, I realized that this was not the case. The opening line was a trick:

I was going to purchase a tarot card reading to tell you this, but I do not want to take up your time. From a business standpoint, you should know that you will not attract many potential clients by saying negative and hurtful things about them.

When the Sun is in reverse, the red, unfurling banner on the card may be a warning. Despite everything looking happy, there is important news. The Sun calls attention and puts the spotlight on something. Sometimes the Sun brings us news we don't want. For instance,

Apollo, the mythological god of light whose symbol is the sun, forced Oedipus to discover the truth about himself.

Uh-oh! Who was this? What did I say? I read on . . .

In December, you gave the man I was seeing a tarot card reading. You told him that I was not the love of his life and that we were not compatible. You said I was very immature, lost in life, and that I don't make smart decisions. You said that he was going to meet the right person at a party. He dumped me after that reading.

I searched my mind over who this man could be. I can speak with twenty or more people a week, outside of working parties and events. I don't keep notes on anyone, as I want to be unbiased and operate from pure intuition. I also don't tell people how to live; I share what I see and let them decide for themselves.

After the incredible grief of December, we got back together. We had too much to lose, you see. Everything was beautiful and happy until now, as we broke up again after his last reading with you yesterday.

Ah! Yesterday. *Yesterday's* clients I could figure out. I looked down my calendar and knew instantly—this was a reading I had done by video conference for Robert, my old teenage boyfriend in Washington, D.C. We stay in touch and catch up every six months or so. Often, I'll give him a reading during those times. Robert had asked me about this girl, Miranda, whom he had been seeing off and on on the heels of breaking up with his long-time girlfriend, Sandy. Sandy broke his heart, so Robert saw Miranda only very casually, in between trying to patch things up with Sandy. That's how he explained it, anyway.

"Miranda shows up with rather unstable energy . . . like a kid," I had said to Robert, holding up a Page of Wands in reverse to the camera on my computer monitor.

The Sun card pictures a happy, naked baby riding a white pony. Children and playfulness are a component of this card. Alchemists refer to the sun as a symbol for transforming base metals into gold; this is sometimes called the Golden Child or the Philosopher's Stone. The Sun card represents it all. I think now of lines in the poem "Lady

Lazarus" by Sylvia Plath: "The pure gold baby / That melts to a shriek."* Plath nailed the Sun in reverse.

Robert responded, "Miranda is a lot younger. In her thirties. That might also refer to the fact that she has kids. Honestly, Julia, I never had kids and don't want to start now. I'm almost sixty. I want to run my company and plan my retirement."

It was then that I gave him a little bit of a lecture, teasing, "Robert, at your age, you ought to know that if you're sleeping with someone, she's going to get attached."

Robert looked a little guilty, even over the occasionally frozen pixels of our video chat.

"Yeah, I know she wants more. She comes over to my home, looks around, and says, 'I could live here.' Dropping a hint, you know. I never say anything back."

The gold of the Sun is also symbolic of spiritual and material wealth. In the background of the Sun card is a wall of white bricks. A walled-in city protects the child. Walls are very good at keeping out the undesirables, but they also keep out a lot of the good. While building a very nice life for himself, my old friend Robert had walled himself in.

"I don't think Miranda is a terrible person," I said, surveying the tarot cards I had laid out for her. "But she is scared, a person driven by fear, and she wants security so badly that I think she confuses that with love. You tell me that you know you don't love her. You're using each other, Robert. You deserve to be loved by a woman who is your equal. Someone you love and respect, not someone looking to you to fix everything. We've talked about your rescuer personality in the past. I don't think Miranda is thinking straight, and it is not your job to fix her. It is your job to be happy."

Behind the wall on the Sun card is a field of sunflowers, the ultimate happy blossom, each a bright yellow plate, like its own sun. Sunflowers are heliotropes; they turn their heads toward the sun, and

---

*Sylvia Plath, "Lady Lazarus" in *Ariel: The Restored Edition* (New York: HarperCollins, 2004), 14.

for this reason, they symbolize worship and a turning to the light. Miranda worshipped Robert and wanted him to take over her life so that she would never have to worry again.

I fingered the Sun card then, which had popped out of the deck as I'd been shuffling. As a card of happiness, right side up, we love the Sun. But upside down, it can be full of deception, as the sun can hide behind the clouds—but you always know it's there.

Miranda's email continued to string me up for execution:

You don't take into consideration who is on the other end of your readings. That this is a person with a life and feelings and an identity. In this situation, you were a long-time friend saying very hurtful things about me to my partner without knowing me or without knowing anything about our relationship. To have one of his friends say such negative things about me and tell him he shouldn't be with me before getting to know me is wrong.

I felt guilty. My words had hurt this person I didn't know, and I had no beef with her. And she was right that my sole focus had been on Robert. I had not considered anyone else. But then I thought, *should I?* I mean, a tarot card reading is an intimate connection with an individual. *One person* seeking guidance and doing the inner work of growing on their spiritual path. It is not a politically correct group thing, censored to please everyone and watered down to avoid hurting feelings. All the time, people say to me: *Don't sugarcoat anything. Give it to me straight.* That's what I want to do.

If I address a person's situation, it will include the people around them. No one is entirely alone and untouched by others, and no matter how I slice it, I'm bound to piss somebody off. Aside from the possibility of telling my client something they don't want to hear, I've irritated others by simply existing. I've had people condemn me, believing that I do Satan's work. Everything upsets someone, and it's sometimes hard to know how much truth is OK. I also don't know how much of what I say will be relayed to others, possibly out of context.

No, intuition doesn't necessarily follow social protocol. I make it a general practice to strive not to hurt anyone, yet tarot readings are not one-size-fits-all. They are not even games of chance. For a fleeting moment, I wished that the cards *were* merely the luck of the draw so that I would not have to take responsibility for my words about Miranda. *You got crushed? Sorry, let's shuffle again! Your life is a wreck? Pick a different card!* No, I had to own my readings. The cards are more personal and truthful than that to me.

I said a prayer and wrote Miranda back in the briefest, most caring yet professional fashion I could manage. I told her that she deserved to be loved properly—not picked up and put down by Robert at a whim. I assured her that I had no romantic motives, which she had alluded to, in my reading for Robert, and that we have been friends for forty years, so my allegiance remains with him. I wished her well and sent her peace. That was all I needed to say. I didn't want to string out her suffering, or let this take up my time, any longer than I had to.

It felt cold yet satisfying for me to write that I did not want to be a part of this and that I was finished talking to her. Just as Robert was now learning, nor did I have to rescue Miranda. In previous years I might have felt an obligation to try to comfort her through her dark time. I have learned the hard way that this never works. Rescuers end up tired, resentful, and used. I've had too many people come to me with anger like this, or making their sad, desperate appeals in the belief that I am the only one able to fix them. We can only fix ourselves, of course. Today, I do not try to fix anyone but myself.

Miranda wrote me back almost immediately. She was angry with me and obsessed with Robert. She argued with my words, saying that I was wrong and that she and Robert unequivocally loved each other. Robert didn't know the depths of his love yet, Miranda believed, and he would learn one day soon that he wanted to have a permanent committed relationship with her. She went back and forth, quoting my words to me in a bold font and then refuting them like questions on a test with her bizarre, manipulative reasoning. I did not respond.

The Sun is the center of the universe upon which the planets of our solar system revolve. It controls the zodiac signs and is the center of creativity in the tarot. Because of this, the Sun may be seen as a card of ego and arrogance. Its movements, storms, and eclipses are closely observed, and its loss is deeply feared. Robert was Miranda's sun, moon, and stars. And Miranda was pretty pissed that he did not hold her in the same regard.

Later that same day, another letter came. Now Miranda sought to bring me to her side. She and I needed to be friends because we both loved Robert, she said. Miranda had been reading my blog and wrote a lengthy treatise on my spiritual observations, pointing out where we agreed and where we were opposed. Miranda's new writing voice was a cocky alter ego, overconfident and declaring that she would have Robert back as soon as he returned to his senses. Again, I did not respond.

And then another email: Miranda pitied Robert, explaining his extreme neediness. She called him schizophrenic. *I'm trying to get you to understand, if you care for Robert, that he is best off with me,* she wrote.

Her final letter to me that day was a total collapse. *Don't you understand how much I need him?* She told me about family tragedies and how everything went wrong. About her failed marriage and a child with autism. How I had made it so much worse.

I could only bring myself to glance at that last email. It drained me to think about it. It drains me to write of it now. The rays of the Sun on the tarot card alternate between straight and squiggly lines representing the masculine and feminine. The golden yellow of the sun symbolizes the heat of emotion. The blue sky behind it is said to represent cool and calm intellect. Together, these colors are the marriage of intellect and emotion, creating the hazardous alchemical process of transmutation for spiritual enlightenment—our pure gold baby, pictured riding on the white horse.

The following day I received a friend request from Miranda on Facebook. Friends?! I ignored it. I began to understand precisely how accurate my original readings for Robert had been. I felt sad for her, having bared all her hurt to me, a perfect stranger. She was so vulnerable and alone. But she had done this relationship with Robert to herself, and she was the only one who could free herself from her personal hell by letting him go and getting on with her life.

The next day, Robert texted me: *Did you call me at 4:00 a.m. this morning?*

I answered: *No! I wouldn't do that!*

That's what I thought, he texted back. Robert said he had been in a dead sleep. He wrote, *Someone, I think we know who, pretended to be you.*

In winter the sun appears to die in the Northern Hemisphere, which we mark by the winter solstice. Similarly it returns at the spring equinox and that "rebirth" has been celebrated since ancient times. The position of the Sun card in the tarot suggests that the Fool has emerged from the underworld with truth, clarity, and sureness.

Robert and I don't talk so much on the phone that he could be sure to know my voice in that foggy, half-awake state. Miranda might have counted on that. He went on to explain that Miranda even took the trouble to get a St. Louis area code phone number to be convincing. Robert had blocked Miranda's usual phone number, although he said she was calling him from other phones.

Impersonated! That was a first. As Robert explained it, Miranda said, pretending to be me, that I had been hired by Robert's old girlfriend Sandy to lie to him about his readings. This was insane. Well, Robert knew that wasn't true, of course, but he put her to the test.

"If this is Julia, what is the nickname I gave you?"

Of course, she didn't know it, because there had never been one.

I thought about Miranda then as the Sun in reverse, cloaking herself behind the clouds of subterfuge while everyone knows it's her. I thought about the intensity and burnout of a reversed Sun and the spotlight of the Sun right side up. Being in the spotlight is only a happy experience some of the time. Impersonation was a new kind of fame, and I didn't want it.

Sometimes, You'll Get Things Wrong

As a tarot card reader or as a human being, I'm not perfect. Is anyone? Sometimes I get things wrong, although my regular clients tell me I am mostly right, and they keep coming back. I have a rotten sense of *gaydar,* for instance, and that Lovers card in the tarot usually shows a heterosexual match to my brain unless I'm using a specialized deck such as the Cosmic Tribe, which has three variations of the Lovers card (traditional, just men, and just women) to accommodate most matchings. But love is love, right? I hope that if my clients miss my not seeing their orientations or other specific details, they still get the overall message and apply it to themselves.

We are, of course, limited by our own experiences. I will probably not get precise health details in medical jargon, as I am not a doctor. Although it would not be out of the realm of possibility for me to say something in a vocabulary that makes no sense to me but makes perfect sense to the person for whom I am reading.

Don't overthink things. The poet Allen Ginsberg popularized the phrase "First thought, best thought" to describe a way to capture truth and fearlessness in writing. That is true with intuition too, which is why intuition and the arts, and especially poetry, are close kin.

20
JUDGEMENT

The first time that Brenda called me, she was frantic. I would soon learn that frantic was her style. She sobbed and said something about how her children wouldn't speak to her and that she was alienated from her grandchildren. "What did I do?" she sobbed. And then, answering her own question, "I didn't do anything!"

Judgement is a card of surveying our lives and our experiences and being accountable for our actions. Mysticism posits that our lives are a creation of our thoughts. Judgement forces us to own this.

My schedule was pretty full. The Easter holiday weekend was coming up, which was in line with Judgement's meaning of rebirth and resurrection. I had eye surgery on the calendar in the next week and a two-week vacation out of the country the week after that. Most of my tarot reading openings were booked, and I wasn't seeking overtime. I've come to a point in my career where I can choose not to work that hard. Phone readings take less time than in-person, but I needed some personal time before my surgery and the trip.

"I want to see you in person!" she urged. "I have seen you before, and I prefer face-to-face."

I didn't want to do it.

"I'm sorry, Brenda, but I can't."

"Do phone readings work just as well?"

"Absolutely. I have many regular phone clients who have never met me in person. So you want a phone reading then?"

Why did I ask her that? I had wondered out loud if I could swing one for her or not, and this was practically an invitation. I regretted the words as soon as they came out of my mouth. At least I could stay home and wouldn't have to get dressed.

The Judgement card can be a struggle to interpret. Depending on its position, some tarot readers say it's about using wise or poor judgment. Had I used poor judgment? In the picture on the card, the red cross on the angel's flag represents many things: it is the flag of St. George, the warrior saint, and patron saint of England. It is the Knights Templar's flag and the Imperial War Flag for the Holy Roman Empire. It symbolizes the martyr's idea of taking up a cross.

It was a Friday night, and I am usually not available for one-on-one sessions on weekends because that is prime time for working larger events. But with the Easter holiday, I had the weekend off to relax. Or so I thought. A reading that night was not resting for me, but Brenda seemed pretty sad, and maybe I could help. I would take up the cross.

"I'd be glad to talk to you tonight on the phone. How about 8:00 p.m.?"

"Great. Thank you so much. I'll call you then."

On the face of the Judgement card is a family, looking cold, naked, and gray-skinned, rising out of icy coffins toward God's Archangel Michael, who calls them to meet their maker. *Michael* means "Who is like God," so his work on the Judgement card can be administering karma, ensuring that one gets what they deserve. Michael carries the souls of the deceased to Heaven, and it is said that he gives each soul an hour to redeem itself. Perhaps I'd redeem myself by giving Brenda an hour of my schedule. It was a sacrifice, but worth it to help someone.

I had seen examples of the alienation of grandparents before with friends and other clients. When a mother or father has a falling out with their grown kids, it is agony when the kids keep the grandchildren from them. It is the meanest kind of revenge, and it hurts the children too. My heart went out to her.

About twenty minutes before my scheduled session with her, one of my best regular clients called and asked if I had any time. I apologized and said, no, not that evening. I was booked.

At 8:00 p.m., my calendar informed me that it was time for Brenda on my schedule. I waited for ten minutes and there was still no call. I sent her a text message: *Waiting on your call.*

No response. Damn it. Brenda had stood me up. And I had turned down my other client! I was mad at myself. The energy hadn't felt right from the start with her. Brenda was pushy, and I had allowed myself to be pushed.

In the Bible the karma of the Judgement card (tarot card twenty) is illustrated with the Bible quote seen earlier in this book for the Wheel of Fortune (card ten): *as you sow, so you shall reap.* The Judgement card packs twice the punch here. What we sow are seeds, of course. Positive seeds blossom. Negative seeds either don't grow, or they give us weeds. Our initial attitude toward something is the seed, that first energy. My attitude toward Brenda had been negative from the start. I should have paid attention. I got my karma.

I let it go and enjoyed my Easter weekend. Brenda called a few times, but I let the phone ring. I didn't want to deal with her. Her voice mails stacked up, each one sounding more breathless and upset than the last:

Hi Julia, this is Brenda. Yes, I would still like a reading. Unfortunately, things are really a mess at the moment and I have no money, so I have to put it off for a little while, but I definitely want to schedule. I would prefer it in person, so give me a call and I will see you when you can get things set up for me, OK? Thank you so much.

Hi Julia, this is Brenda. I know we've been having trouble connecting. I am very interested in seeing you, whatever time of day or location is convenient for you. Please give me a call back. I implore you. I need very much to speak with you and set up a reading. I don't mean to pressure you, but time is of the essence. I will probably be leaving this area in May, so please get back in touch with me as soon as possible. I much appreciate it. Thank you.

I would not answer. There had been no apology, only accelerated demands. By now, I had an attitude. "We teach the world how to treat us," I tell my clients, "by what we put up with." I had already put up with too much.

The Wednesday after Easter, Brenda texted me. It was as if she had only just read my "Waiting on your call" message from a week earlier. She responded with: *Yes, are you available tonight at about 9 or 10 p.m.?*

I answered by text:

Hi Brenda, sorry, but I was busy over Easter weekend. I don't make appointments as late as 9—too exhausting. I've got in-person sessions that will keep me busy until 8:30 tonight. And I don't want to schedule with you if you won't do it. I turned someone down last Friday night because I'd saved that time for you.

There was no response back. Good. I didn't want to talk to Brenda again.

A few days went by, and it was the weekend again. My phone rang, and without considering who might be calling, I picked it up.

"Hello, this is Julia."

"Julia, this is Brenda. Sorry we keep missing each other. Hey, I really need to see you. Time is running out. I've got an emergency here. . . ."

I cringed. Missing each other? I hadn't been missing her. I had been avoiding her. And she hadn't communicated back to me anyway.

"Um, did you get the text messages I sent to you?" I asked.

"Yes. Listen, I need to see you in person. I've got terminal cancer, and everything's going wrong, and it's important I get in with you soon. I didn't call last week because I didn't have the money, but I have it now."

There is only one other tarot card in the Major Arcana where we see a man, woman, and child pictured together: the Death card. Judgement tells us that they rise to embrace their new lives and a new calling. It is a card of rebirth and resurrection. *A Course in Miracles* declares that if we remove our opinions of guilt about other people, we remove them from ourselves.

I knew that I held Brenda in my mind as guilty. She was driving me freaking crazy. Some clients bowl me over with their drama. Yes, it's all sad: alienation from her grandchildren, cancer, money problems. Who knows what else? But there was this lack of respect, no apologies, and no effort to make it right. And her demands on my time. And there I was, with my problems of the privileged, it was true, now three days from my vacation with an ice pack on my face to keep the bruising and swelling down from my recent eye surgery. However, I have been on the other end, in a scary place of no health insurance and no money for necessities. Of years without being able to take vacations. I have suffered over family. Maybe I should understand that she might not be coming from a place of politeness and respect because she doesn't have the tools right now. I didn't have the strength to fight with her.

"Brenda, I am in no condition to be seen in public. I look like I've been through a war."

"That's OK! I've got cancer! I'm a mess too. Let me come to your house then. I'll drive anywhere. I need to see you, Julia. *Please.*"

"I have very little time, Brenda. I am trying to get a lot of things done before I leave. . . ."

"Please! I'll come at any time that is convenient for you. And I have the money."

I gave her my home address and told her to come at 11:00 a.m. the following day. We hung up the phone and I immediately began to cogitate over how I got talked into that. I walked a confusing tight-rope between compassion for her and compassion for myself. Some people are not right for us, and boundaries are essential.

That night I laid awake, wishing I'd never given her my address. I didn't need the money that badly. She was not mentally stable. She may not be safe. Why did I do it?

Some see the cross on the flag on the Judgement card as a crossroads or a meeting of opposites. It is also seen as a joining of things that had been separated, including of the souls with God. The cross also represents the juncture of two kinds of time: the ordinary and the eternal.

Monday morning, I went walking with my friend Judy to get the first half of my 10,000 steps in for the day. Judy is my sounding board, and she is full of wisdom.

"I don't know how I got so bamboozled," I told her. "This woman has been nothing but disrespectful to me, and now she is coming over today." I filled her in on how Brenda plowed right over everything I had to say.

"She didn't apologize for standing you up or say that she would try to make it right?"

"No. Not even when I told her that I turned down another client for her."

"Julia, you need to cancel with her. You don't need that woman in your home."

"I know that my energy is wrong over this. I know that I am angry and resentful. But I guess I feel sorry for Brenda too."

"Well, Brenda sure didn't feel sorry for you, did she?"

"I suppose not. It's hard for me to say no for some reason."

"Julia, I'll tell you why it's hard for you. Because you're used to accepting abuse and disrespect. A person who is used to being respected would not put up with this. Cancel that job with her, and don't give her a reason. Explaining yourself makes you do the helpless victim crap. You decide how to react, and you can decide not to give her power. Cancel it because you want to cancel it."

"Oh, Judy. I can't do that. I have to give her at least a reason."

"She didn't give you that much last week, did she?"

"No. It's just . . . I don't know. I am better than that. I'll take the job. I could use the money before I leave town."

"Don't do it, Julia. You said yourself your energy wouldn't be right for her anyway. You won't be able to help her at all."

"I know. Brenda feels like a vampire. Just talking about her exhausts me."

"So cancel."

"I will. But I am going to explain a little bit as to why."

Judgment day, pictured on the Judgement card, can be the soul's descent into Hell as easily as being called to Heaven. The Archangel Michael is fierce and uncompromising. We have been on this journey through the tarot's Major Arcana, being tested and experiencing life's challenges. Judgement is about acknowledging and assimilating our lessons before the cycle begins again. Because otherwise, we will get the same old story, over and over, until it finally gets through. If I didn't get this lesson, this gift of Brenda doing this to me, how many more times would the situation repeat? The journey into the abyss was my own, not Brenda's.

I texted her: *Hi Brenda. After Friday's no-show and no apology, I don't want to work with you. Please consider today and future appointments canceled.*

"There," I said to Judy. "Was I owning it there? Not being a victim?"

"Yes, that was good," Judy said. "I bet that now your phone will blow up, and she will not take no for an answer."

Judy proved herself to also be a skillful soothsayer. Not only did Brenda not take no for an answer, but she also did not read or purposefully ignored my texts.

I did not want to be around if or when Brenda came to my home. I taped a note to my locked storm door that read: *Brenda, I sent you a text this morning that I canceled. —Julia*

The Judgement card shows a layer of billowy clouds that separate the upper from the lower world. They show a higher nature that we can't always see in the mundane. I had to keep looking for the blessing. When we are upset or unhappy, *A Course in Miracles* suggests that this is a sign that we are blaming someone else. Forgiveness and seeing the other through God's love is the only way out. But I had to forgive myself for being a doormat too.

There would be no excuses on my part. No victim shit. I knew then that I *was* fearful about what an encounter with Brenda might turn into. I imagined her peeking in through the front door window, seeing a candle burning in my dining room, and knowing I was there. I blew it out. If she was that overexcited on the phone, how might she be if she knew I was avoiding her? I did not feel safe working in my office beside the front door as she might hear me typing or see movement through the blinds. I locked the back door and double-checked the sliding glass door on the deck. What was I afraid of? Being attacked? Maybe. I'm adept in the spiritual world, but I suck at the physical. The conversation was all a little too obsessive and over-wrought with her. I decided it would be a good time to leave and get my nails done, something on my to-do list before leaving for vaca-tion. I got in my car and sped away to the safety of the world outside my home.

At 11:15 a.m., my phone rang, and I sent it to voice mail. I lis-tened later:

Julia, It's Brenda. I'm sorry, but I'm running late. Things are crazy, and I couldn't get out in enough time, but I will be there soon.

Shit. Brenda hadn't read my text. And look at that! She would have been late if I *had* been waiting. In the nail salon, I turned my ringer off. I would treasure my little hour of peace. When I got back to my car, I looked, and there were three more messages:

Julia, I'm sorry. I'm at the ATM, and I am having problems get-ting the money. I really want to see you, and I was wondering if you could . . . well, never mind. Let me try and get this. I'll be there soon.

Now she would try to guilt me into not charging her too. And if she was having such money problems, why was she getting a tarot reading?

Hi Julia, it's Brenda again. I have your money, and I am on my way. But I can't find the text with your address. I remember the general area, and I am headed there, but can you call me back or text me the address?

Hi Julia. I am waiting for you to text me your address. I am close.

If she had lost my address, there was no way that I would give it to her again. She seemed selective about the text messages she was willing to receive. She had certainly seen, or been able to see, that I canceled with her earlier. No, she bulldozed right over my cancellation, the way that she had bulldozed me when we were on the phone.

It was now past one thirty; I had made another appointment with a regular client who is considerate and appreciative of my time. He reminded me of the things I love about my work, and we laughed and enjoyed the session. I was not going to waste another minute with Brenda.

I texted her a reply to her many messages: *Brenda, I don't have time for this. I have too much to do and feel forced into this. My energy is wrong now, and I wouldn't give you a good reading because it is rushed and inconvenient. I need my clients to respect me, give advance notice when they can't make it, and be on time. I cannot fix you, and I feel like you are expecting too much from me when you must work on yourself. I can't heal you.*

It felt honest to write it. I can love Brenda—from a distance— but the only way I can help her is to work on myself. When I treat myself as a child of God, everyone else who touches me in this world will benefit, including Brenda. We must forgive everyone, but we are not required to tell them, and forgiveness does not mean they must remain in our lives. I slowed down and looked at how I had participated in this ridiculous scenario, which ultimately took up most of my morning and early afternoon. I got interested in my own behavior. Why couldn't I have said, "Sorry, not today," and hung up with no guilt from me or judgment toward her? Why did I have to jump into this escalation that made her the bad guy in order to accept my own emotions?

Several years ago, I had a meditation day with some friends. It was a full day of fasting, meditation, and prayer in a dark room in the yoga *savasana*, known as the "corpse pose." This practice was far more grueling than one might expect, and it challenged what the Buddhists call my "monkey mind" to stay centered. Eventually, after several hours of breathing and mantra work, I felt a very physical vibration and then the greatest spiritual epiphany I have ever experienced. I was in the presence of God. I asked every question in my thoughts: *Why is there war? Why is there abuse? Why is there suffering?* I got only one answer back for everything: *They forgot. They forgot. They forgot.* And it was then that I understood that we have continually forgotten that we are one and a part of God. We forget all the time with everything that seems to go wrong. The Judgement card proclaims that there is no personal liberation. The mass of people pictured in the distance shows that we raise each other up. Because we are all members of the human race, we are responsible for the entire human race. No one can suffer a problem that will not affect us all energetically, and no one can be liberated from a problem that does not free us all. It was time to free myself of my baggage.

"There seems to be a block in you that keeps reinforcing that you don't matter," Judy had said about the Brenda situation. Yes. I had felt this my whole life. It was time to be done with it. Who said I had to help everyone all the time? I don't have to take on every client who comes to me. It does not make me a terrible person to take care of myself. Helping and honoring myself is part of helping everyone.

I justified all of these things in my head, and then I had to ask: How do I make myself more important than these justifications? What if I don't need a reason to say no? What if feeling like saying no is enough?

I have forever been too polite for my own good. I was even polite to my rapist twenty-five years ago. It is time to be done with all of that. How am I still just learning how to be a competent human being at fifty-five years old? It was then that I understood, in this circumstance, that one of the kindest things I could do for Brenda was to hold her accountable for her behavior, so that she could learn.

I have seen some tarot decks rename the Judgement card as *The Call* or *A Calling.* This is because it is a card that shows us our higher selves and what we must do, what we were made for. As children of God, being a part of God, we can have no dreams or desires that aren't meant to be actualized as long as they contribute positively to the world. I love tarot, writing, and my Sylvia Plath scholarship. These three things are my calling. God found a clever system to give me all three simultaneously. How far I go with these depends on how well I learn my life lessons. And also realizing that any bad feelings or lack of forgiveness I have, for Brenda or anyone else, will hold me back.

I am stepping into a different life for myself, a resurrection, if you will. I can be grateful to Brenda for being the gift to get me there. She showed me how I have been complicit in keeping myself down for more than half a century. I am getting ready to say *yes* to so many new and exciting things. But how can I say a real *yes* if I cannot say a real *no?*

Brenda texted several times after, asking if I might consider a half-hour reading, and did I know of a good healer, she was very sorry to have overwhelmed me, and she had been insensitive about my eyes. *Please let me know if you need anything,* she wrote.

Sorry, no. A real no. Not today. Not anymore.

Step by Step in the Circle of Life

You've seen how each card in the Major Arcana opens the door to the next one. This life story is called the "path of the initiate" in alchemy, or the hero's journey to mythologists such as Joseph Campbell. It is every stage that happens in a human being's life, from birth to death. And we may go through this cycle a couple of times in one life, depending on how much we want to keep learning and grow.

The Judgement card is the second-to-last card in the Major Arcana. It may have been intended to settle all the soul's affairs and get the heart in the right place before we close the door with the World card, and begin again.

21
THE WORLD

It had been a busy Halloween season with a lot of parties. The little country library had me back for the fourth year in a row; last year was a Harry Potter–themed party, and the year before that, I went to a private event at the house of someone connected to the library. The previous year I had presented on the tarot in the library's largest room, which was such a big deal for this small town that even the media was there to cover it. This year was a "Witches Tea." These two librarians were nuts about me and treated me like a celebrity, blowing their budget to book me almost a year in advance. I stood outside the door as Beth, the head librarian, introduced me to her crowded room of participants:

"We have a *very special* guest tonight . . . Julia Gordon-Bramer!" *Applause.*

Too sweet. Like I was Madonna or something. I didn't even mind the hour-long drive each way for a reception like that.

The World card concludes the tarot's Major Arcana. It is a card of success, completion, and self-actualization. Even when it falls in reverse, the World says that we are on that path, only it hasn't happened quite yet.

Over the evening I read for all the participants dressed up as witches and sipping various brews of herbal tea. With their tall hats and black gauzy dresses, spider-bedecked veils, and broomsticks, I got the usual laughs and tears at my table in the hallway, where they positioned me this year to give people their privacy. It had been a fine party, and everyone left satisfied with their readings, even those who didn't know what tarot was about. The librarians paid me a little extra to give them personal readings after the doors closed and the exterior lights were turned out.

The lights were also off in all the back areas, where the books were, and the three of us sat at my table in the front. A single can light illuminated this sublime space from the ceiling. They made me feel so revered, like a wise elder or shaman. But they were also intelligent and strong women. As a writer myself, I felt proud of all they did, devoting their lives to books and literacy.

If you've ever done work with dream analysis, you understand that everything means something. Just as when you dream and your brain codes the events and experiences of the day with strange symbols, so it is with the cards. One day, the World card may represent the world in its most literal meaning. Another day, it may mean worldwide success, and another day, it may mean a loved one who is the whole world to someone. Or it might mean *whirled*—homophones can come into play too. Everything is a clue, and interpreting is a mystical, intuitive game.

Beth went first.

"Beth, you've made a pleasant life for yourself with this Nine of Pentacles, and some luxuries show up here with the Devil. The Emperor tells me that you run a tight ship. The Four of Wands tells me your home is stable, but there is this Four of Swords reversed over you, which is a serious depression in the past. It's still showing up, so you're carrying it along." The Four of Swords looks like a dark crypt for a dead knight.

"What I've never told you over all these years, Julia," Beth said, "was that my son died. About five years ago. You saw things about it every time you read for me, but I never explained."

As on the Wheel of Fortune card, the World has symbolic creatures in all four of its corners, representing all four Archangels (Raphael is Aquarius, the man; Gabriel is Scorpio, the eagle; Uriel is Taurus, the Bull; and Michael is Leo, the Lion). These symbols also represent the four fixed signs of the zodiac, the four cardinal directions of a compass, and the four living creatures of the Apocalypse. While the Wheel of Fortune is the more everyday good luck card, the World is a significant accomplishment or achievement. It can also be closing a door when life, or a period of life, is over.

"Oh, Beth. I'm so sorry. *Of course* that is depression you would carry along. One doesn't just get over that. Would you like me to look at your son?"

"Could we?"

"Yes. I don't conduct a back and forth conversation with the cards. I will ask and see if there are any messages for you. How does that sound?"

I never thought of reading tarot cards for people who had passed on until some of my clients urged me to try. Then they told me how I said something just the way the person who had passed used to say it, or that I named a specific color, or described their car, or something unique. I validated that the soul of a loved one was there. Sometimes I didn't even know that the person had died. Clients became so passionate about what I saw that now reading for those who have passed on is part of my repertoire.

Beth nodded that she wanted me to do this.

"What's his name?"

"Charles," she said.

On the face of the World card is a picture of a naked dancing woman, wearing only a veil. She dances in the center of an oval wreath, said to represent the female womb. The World is the portal back to God before returning to a new life in the Fool card. It is considered a celebration of life and an understanding of all things.

When I put down Beth's cards, I saw the wild energy of the Page of Wands reversed, followed by the Eight of Swords reversed. "Charles is telling me he has been freed from a behavior problem of some kind. It has been driven out of him now, and he is his authentic self."

"Charles had autism," she said, looking relieved to think that he does not have to suffer that on the other side. Autism is, of course, a constraint of the body, not the soul. "He had a seizure and hit his head against the bed's headboard. I know I shouldn't judge myself, but I can't help it. We didn't find him until morning, when it was too late. He was sixteen."

I reached over and squeezed her hand. Then I laid down some more cards for her.

"The Empress and the Strength card! The Empress is the great mother, and his love for you is still strong, Beth. You're not alone. He is still with you." Tears filled her eyes.

I continued, "The Tower, the Ten of Swords, and the Fool card . . . I think he died suddenly and felt nothing. And now, if you believe in reincarnation, which many of us do, his spirit will come back again. Maybe next time, he will get to enjoy more blessings. That is what we will pray for, right?"

Alchemists see the naked dancing woman on the World card as the Hermaphrodite, the perfect combination of male and female, as a symbol of joining the conscious with the subconscious, or the Philosopher's Child. It is this blending that creates perfection.

Next, it was the turn of the other librarian, Susan. Her cards were morose and full of sadness: the Three of Swords, the Four of Swords, the Ten of Cups in reverse, the Death card, and the World in reverse.

"Susan, the Death card rarely means actual death, but it looks like you might have had a death in the family with these other cards around it."

She nodded. "My niece. My three-month-old niece died from SIDS last month." She started to cry.

"Oh, God. I am so sorry. You two have a lot of suffering between you, huh?"

They both looked at each other and tried to smile. Beth put a hand on Susan's shoulder.

"Would you like us to look at this baby too?" I asked Susan, unsure if it might be too soon. Susan said yes, and told me that her departed niece's name was Laurie. I had Susan shuffle again, back and forth, stacking and restacking them. I told her to think of Laurie.

I had become a bridge to the other side. Or not a bridge, exactly, because a bridge connects land to land. I join the rugged and rational land to the watery subconscious. I teach people how to dip their toes into the water and get wet in the feeling. In the World card, the woman pictured is a soul celebrating her time in the world of sensation, intoxicated by the joy of human life and expression.

The cards I put down were unexpected: the Knight of Cups, the Devil, the Ace of Cups, and the World. I smiled, and then I actually began to laugh a little, although my eyes were wet with tears.

"I can hardly believe this, Susan. I've never had a reading like this one before in over forty years of reading the tarot. Here is what I see from little Laurie:

"'My life was great!' The Knight of Cups says she knows that she was wanted and loved. The Devil card says she had everything she wanted and more. It was fun! And if you believe in reincarnation, the Ace of Cups seems as if she's saying, 'I'll come back again.' Her last card, the World, shows that she believes her life was successful and complete."

Susan smiled and laughed a little, admitting that the baby's life had been precisely that.

The World tells us that all things eventually come to an end and that from every ending comes a new beginning.

"I know it isn't easy, but try not to be too sad. Her life was perfect. Who are we to say that a life isn't fantastic and well lived if it ends at three months, or sixteen years, or one hundred and twenty years? Their work is done when it's done. Maybe Laurie simply wanted to have that life experience of being born and loved. Perhaps that little bit of a great life was enough for her. Reincarnation is in all the major religions except Christianity. It used to be in Christianity until Emperor Constantine removed mention of it from the Bible because he didn't want people thinking they could disobey the church and get another chance. My point being that Laurie may even return. Maybe in your lifetime, or maybe she'll wait for you and you will go to the next one together. In any case, Laurie is in the revolving door. That body you met is over, but *she* isn't over.

"We are here to put on these masks and play these roles for however long our part in the play of life lasts. We all have soul contracts. For instance, Charles said, 'I'll play the boy with autism,' and Laurie said, 'And I'll be the baby who dies.' But this is not the truth of them or us. The truth is that we're all connected to the God source, that life force that's waiting in the wings. Energy doesn't die. Science has proven that. Our bodies crap out on us, but energy goes somewhere else. The truth is that Charles never intrinsically left, nor did Laurie. They're just waiting on the other side for us to finish with our parts here on Earth."

After the World card, we come full circle in the Major Arcana to begin it again. That's all we do in these lives—go round and round.

I got in my car, opened my notebook, and jotted down the main ideas that would become this final story because I knew it was too meaningful to forget. As I finished writing Charles's and Laurie's stories, my son called me to say hi, and I felt blessed beyond belief that my kids made it to adulthood and are happy and healthy.

I started down that long dark highway, north and east toward St. Louis, remembering a spiritual experience I had a few years earlier: I woke up with a vision of a sign carved in wood: *Trust. You've Already Become.*

I try to remember this. Do we look at a newborn baby and say, "Eh, not quite. She needs better hair, or a better body, or let's have her do something worthwhile first, to be lovable"? Of course not. A newborn baby just *is*. And like a newborn baby, we are all the same person we were on the day we were born. Today we are bigger, and we have more stories—and a whole lot of layers of false beliefs to peel away. It's not that we have to become anything. We are already everything. We just need to find it again.

The Tao Te Ching says: "See the world as yourself. Have faith in the way things are. Love the world as yourself; then you can care for all things." Tarot helps me to do this. Maybe it will help you too.

Tarot for Creativity

There are other uses for the tarot beyond just understanding a situation, knowing what's going on with someone else, or determining one's future. Tarot cards are terrific creative tools for writers and artists. I know many creative people who pull a card for inspiration or to help them take a project in a new direction. Tarot can be used to influence situations, with yourself and with others, by helping to clarify beliefs, habits, and energetic patterns. We come to the tarot to find language for the impenetrable emotions and things we don't have language for. As they say: *A picture says a thousand words*. Let tarot show you your next steps in life and how you might create it.

RESOURCES

I have hundreds of tarot decks. Some are very collectible and rare, such as Salvador Dali's *Tarot Universal Dali* in its suede box (Comas), or the long out-of-print *Astral Tarot* (Mont-Saint-Johns) from 1969. Ed Buryn's *William Blake Tarot* (HarperCollins) is fascinating, as this famous poet/artist basically intuited the tarot system long before it had come to his home country of England. I've got many cat decks (my spirit animal), but Lunaea Weatherstone and Mickie Mueller's *Mystical Cats Tarot* (Llewellyn) is my favorite of all of them. I've even got rock and roll–themed tarot decks. Davide De Angelis's David Bowie–inspired *Starman Tarot* (Lo Scarabeo), anyone?

These collectible decks, however, are put away to admire and not what I use for day-to-day readings (frequent use wears out the cards and these decks must be replaced regularly). Here are my go-to decks for client work:

Universal Waite Tarot (U.S. Games Systems)—This deck is best for beginners, with all of the Rider-Waite symbolism I refer to in this book.

The Alchemical Tarot: Renewed by Robert M. Place (Hermes Publications)—The now out-of-print 1994–2007 version is my favorite, with brighter colors (please bring this back, Robert!). Clients have expressed that this deck looks very much like tattoo art. I adore Place's take on some of these cards, such as the Five of Cups, which opened up and expanded meanings for me as a reader.

The Hermetic Tarot (U.S. Games Systems)—With a box framed in bright red, this black-and-white deck seems to call to men especially. I have had clients say, "I have black-and-white questions; I want black-and-white answers." Others find its starkness scary. I like to have it as an option.

Mystic Mondays Tarot by Grace Duong (Chronicle Books)—The vibrant colors, the clean, modern design, and feminist vibes are irresistible. A client favorite.

Joie de Vivre Tarot by Paulina Cassidy (U.S. Games Systems)—I call this one my "Tim Burton deck." It has no connection with the famous filmmaker, but Joie de Vivre has the same kind of weird, playful vibe. My clients have loved this deck for many years.

Shadowscapes Tarot by Stephanie Pui-Mun Law (Llewellyn)—For readers who want even the more difficult cards to look soft and beautiful, this deck is for you. Also popular with fairy fans.

Star Spinner Tarot by Trungles (Chronicle Books)—Clients enjoy the art deco design of these cards, as well as an inclusive mix with multiple versions of the Lovers card. My only complaint is the very small print, which can be hard on aging eyes, especially when the imagery is not always in alignment with the traditional Rider-Waite symbolism. But clients love this deck!

Cosmic Tarot by Norbert Lösche (AGM Urania/U.S. Games Systems)—Very close to the classical Rider-Waite deck in symbolism, the Cosmic Tarot kicks the colors up a notch and the representations of people, especially, are very good.

ACKNOWLEDGMENTS

This book was my husband, Tom Bramer's, idea and would not have happened if not for his suggestion. It would also have been impossible to write this without the stories of my tarot clients who opened up their personal lives to me, a complete stranger, and let the cards reveal all that they could not say. I have made every effort to conceal personal facts and respect privacy while still sharing their important and universal stories.

I have so much gratitude, to Casey Hampton and Ti Sumner for their early reading and terrific comments on the first draft. To Susan McBride, my friend and an amazing author of fiction and nonfiction, who valiantly pitched this to her agency, but they were just not quite ready for such a weird subject as this! To Zulfikar Ghose, my best critic, mentor, and friend, who read a number of early versions of these stories in his emails from me.

Thank you to the great poet and my dear friend Matthew Freeman who gets a mention in the Moon story; to Tero Goldenhill, the Finnish card reader who read for me at Treadwell's in London in the Emperor story; and Judy Ryan of LifeworkSystems, who shows up in the Judgement card tale. In chapter 9's text box, the reader using "messy piles" is author/tarot reader Michael M. Hughes, who says this is called the *open* method of reading tarot cards, a term coined by Yoav Ben-Dov in his book *Tarot: The Open Reading* (CreateSpace, 2013).

I have so much appreciation for NewsTalkSTL 101.9 and 94.1 FM for inviting me to bring my radio program, *Mystic Fix,* to their airwaves (podcast and videocast too); and to my sponsor KAMAFLIGHT and its creator, Roland Peralta, for making this program possible.

Thanks to my family and especially my little sister Kristina Morgan who refers to me as "The Oracle," and keeps the faith and the laughter. I also must thank the still-powerful energy of Sylvia Plath because if it were not for all of my scholarship on her over these past two decades, I would not be half as knowledgeable about tarot and Qabalah. Simply put: Plath made me a better tarot card reader. Much appreciation also for the women in my Wisdom group and my A Course in Miracles community. Both meetings are vitally important to me, teach me, and sustain me. I'm incredibly grateful to Tamra Lucid, a fellow Plath fan and angel out of nowhere (Instagram!), for my initial introduction to acquisitions editor Jon Graham. Jon, Erica Robinson, Jamaica Burns Griffin, Manzanita Carpenter Sanz, and all the staff at Inner Traditions have been a joy to work with. Finally, thanks to Spirit, who channeled this whole thing through me in diary entries over the years and made it so easy to pull together. The God stuff always does seem to flow that way.

You can find me on Twitter and Instagram at @jgordonbramer or @mystic_fix to say hello.

INDEX